GROVE PRESS MODERN DRAMATISTS

Grove Press Modern Dramatists
Series Editors: *Bruce King* and *Adele King*

Published titles

Neil Carson, *Arthur Miller*
Ruby Cohn, *New American Dramatists, 1960–1980*
Bernard F. Dukore, *Harold Pinter*
Julian Hilton, *Georg Büchner*
Leonard C. Pronko, *Eugène Labiche and Georges Feydeau*
Theodore Shank, *American Alternative Theater*

Further titles in preparation

GROVE PRESS MODERN DRAMATISTS

GEORG BÜCHNER

by **Julian Hilton**

Lecturer in Drama
University of East Anglia

Grove Press, Inc., New York

First published 1982 by The Macmillan Press Ltd.,
London and Basingstoke.

First Evergreen Edition 1982
First Printing 1982
ISBN: 0–394–17967–6
Library of Congress Catalog Card Number: 81–84702

Printed in Hong Kong

GROVE PRESS, INC., 196 West Houston Street, New York, N.Y. 10014

Contents

List of Plates

List of Plates

5. Claus Eberth (*c.*) as Danton in *Danton's Death*, Kammerspiele Munich 1980, directed by Dieter Dorn. The waxwork group (*l.*) represents Danton, La Marseillaise and Robespierre. Photograph: Rabanus

6. Albrecht Peter as Wozzeck and Elisabeth Lindermeier as Marie in *Wozzeck*, the opera by Alban Berg, Prinzregententheater Munich 1957, conducted by Ferenc Fricsay, directed by Rudolf Hartmann, designed by Helmut Jürgens. Photograph: Sabine Toepffer

7. Diego Leon as President, Wolfram Mehring as Leonce and Grillon as Valerio in *Leonce and Lena*, directed by Wolfram Mehring, Theéâtre Franco-Allemand, Paris 1959. Photograph: Etienne Weill

8. The Gate Theatre production of *Leonce and Lena*, London 1980, directed by Nick Hamm

Acknowledgements

It gives me great pleasure to thank all those who have helped me write this book: to Oberbürgermeister Anno Vey and Schiedsmann Willi Laufersweiler for the generous provision of office accommodation in the Old Town Hall, Ingelheim and to the archivist Herr Gaul for his help; to my mother-in-law, Elsbeth Boenisch, for keeping house; to my wife, Hanne, for teaching me German and listening to all the drafts; to my colleagues Tony Gash, Nicholas Brooke and, especially, Tony Frost for countless ideas and suggestions; to Nick Hamm for working on *Leonce and Lena*; to the University of East Anglia for granting me study leave; to the General Editor, Bruce King, for invaluable editorial advice. To one man, however, my thanks go in particular, Dr Anton Büchner: in providing me with his own archive material, his writings about Georg and the whole Büchner family and with a great deal of his time in seeing through the drafts and the translations. His contribution both to the text of this book and to its background is incalculable. If I have succeeded in conveying the spirit of his great-uncle Georg it is largely his doing.

Ingelheim/Rhein.

Note on Translations

All the translations in this book, with the exception of passages from Aristotle's *Poetics*, are my own. I have used the Everyman edition of the *Poetics*, to which the reader is referred. Quotations from Büchner are from *Georg Büchner sämtliche Werke und Briefe* (*Historisch-kritische Ausgabe mit Kommentar*), 4 vols, edited by Werner R. Lehmann (Christian Wegner Verlag: Hamburg, 1967).

Editors' Preface

The *Grove Press Modern Dramatists* is an international series of introductions to major and significant nineteenth and twentieth century dramatists, movements and new forms of drama in Europe, Great Britain, America and new nations such as Nigeria and Trinidad. Besides new studies of great and influential dramatists of the past, the series includes volumes on contemporary authors, recent trends in the theatre and on many dramatists, such as writers of farce, who have created theatre 'classics' while being neglected by literary criticism. The volumes in the series devoted to individual dramatists include a biography, a survey of the plays, and detailed analysis of the most significant plays, along with discussion, where relevant, of the political, social, historical and theatrical context. The authors of the volumes, who are involved with theatre as playwrights, directors, actors, teachers and critics, are concerned with the plays as theatre and discuss such matters as performance, character interpretation and staging, along with themes and contexts.

Editors' Preface

Grove Press Modern Dramatists are written for people interested in modern theatre who prefer concise, intelligent studies of drama and dramatists, without jargon and an excess of footnotes.

BRUCE KING
ADELE KING

1
A Brief Life: 1813-37

Few mysteries of life are more impenetrable and none causes deeper grief than the death of the young. When such a young person has one of the most brilliant minds and warm personalities of his whole generation that mystery takes on a capricious, even malicious aspect. Death is the single most powerful force in all Georg Büchner's writings, and death claimed him at only twenty-three, as he was coming rapidly to the height of his powers. His originality, neglect and rediscovery lend his life a romantic air but while he understood and was indebted to romanticism he was a realist with a far-seeing literary, political and scientific vision which informs his work even now with freshness and a sense of prophecy.

Büchner is best known as the author of a fragment of a novel, *Lenz* (1836) and three surviving plays, *Danton's Death* (1835), *Leonce and Lena* (1836) and *Woyzeck* (1836/ 7). A fourth play, based on the writings of the sixteenth-century satirist Aretino, his diary, and all or parts of many letters are missing, either burned by his fiancée Minna or

1

censored by his family, worried by the politically sensitive material they very likely contained. What does survive of the overtly political writing is the *Hessian Peasant Courier* (1834) which was the cause of his political exile in 1835.

All these writings are full of complex editorial problems some of which are insoluble and many of which have only very recently been solved. Only *Danton's Death* and the *Courier* were published in Büchner's lifetime, and both were substantially amended from his original drafts. In 1850 his brother Ludwig tried to rectify this by publishing extracts from the surviving papers but he managed in the process to leave out *Woyzeck* entirely and remove any sensitive material from the letters. The one good effect of this editorial travesty was to inspire Karl Emil Franzos to assemble Büchner's manuscripts for a complete edition which was ready in 1879. Franzos had difficulties with Büchner's handwriting and made many mistakes – 'Wozzeck' for 'Woyzeck' being the most famous – but his edition was the beginning of the Büchner revival. This was superseded in 1922 by Fritz Bergemann's edition but where Franzos had committed errors of transcription Bergemann made several of editorial judgement, most notably about the text of *Woyzeck*. It took until 1971 for these errors to be pointed out by Werner Lehmann whose work, still in progress, is the first to conform to the standards of modern editorial practice. It is a mark of the difficulty that attends Büchner studies that only in the last decade has there been a reliable Büchner text.[1]

As well as a dramatist and polemicist Büchner was a scientist and philosopher. He studied medicine at Strasbourg and Giessen and became Reader in Comparative Anatomy at the new University of Zürich aged only 23. His scientific skill in observation and in analysis was such that modern commentators have seen in him a potential Charles

Darwin, whose theories on evolution Büchner's work in some respects anticipated.[2] His contemporaries thought him equally gifted at philosophy, seeing in his essays on Descartes and Spinoza the beginnings of a movement to challenge the all-powerful Hegelians who dominated German intellectual life in the 1830s. Both these aspects of his work give his creative writing its distinctiveness, combining the pathologist's ability to record simply what is there in front of him with the philosopher's preparedness constantly to re-examine the foundations of his subject. Intellectually this places Büchner in the French *philosophe* tradition, a tradition which contributed vitally to the events which most attracted Büchner's historical and political imagination, the French Revolution.

From the warrant issued by the Hessian police as a result of his revolutionary activities we now know what he looked like to the official eye: tall for his time (1.75m), blond, grey-eyed and very short-sighted. His mouth was small and he had a strong, slim figure dominated by a markedly rounded forehead, which gets a special mention.[3]

As well as the warrant, two pictures have survived which illustrate well the critical controversy that still surrounds him. The best known of these is the 'romantic' one, showing a brooding, somewhat melancholy genius with a firm will and a sober if expensive taste in clothes. Very recently the most energetic of all Büchner researchers, Thomas Michael Mayer, has attacked both the picture and the message it conveys and argued most convincingly for a tiny pencil sketch, recently discovered, by Alexis Muston. This is only 4cm high, taken from life during a walking tour in the Odenwald. Here the forehead is almost all the face, which is much thinner and the hair far wilder than on the romantic portrait. There is more of the witty mimic in the eyes, a feature which his friends singled out when talking about him the day after his death.

A glance through my own photo album shows versions of my face just as varied as these, so I am disinclined to accept Mayer's argument that the familiar picture should be totally rejected.[4] But his claim reminds us of the crucial lacunae in the extant Büchner text: there are myths generated about any great writer, but the gaps in Büchner's life and writings give rise to more than most. While it is true that part of his meaning is the myth, there are many issues where the myth and the reality are so far apart that serious damage is done to what he wrote. This problem is most acute when constructing an acceptable *Woyzeck* text, but it is present everywhere. Mayer rightly challenges us to be accurate and unfanciful.

Four major concerns underlie my study, two intrinsic to the works themselves and two specific to the problem of translation.

1) Because there is a gap of half a century between Büchner's writing and the time it began to filter its way into European consciousness – almost a century passed before his work established itself as 'classic' – a study of his work has necessarily two aspects, as product of his own time and as understood by ours. In particular this raises the problem of Büchner's modernity, which I shall consider in my last chapter.

2) There is no evidence that Büchner had any practical stage experience, unlike nearly every other great stage writer, nor did he advance any theory of stagecraft. This raises a distinct possibility that the revolutionary demands he placed on actors and producers were unconscious, which should warn us, when considering claims that he is father of modern western theatre, to tread carefully.

3) German political history, so decisive in the effect Büchner has had on his audiences and readers – and on his

own life – is little understood outside Germany. This means the necessary common sociological base for translation is missing and certain experiences he describes, especially that of absolute government, are unknown at least to many of his English-language readers.

4) Both German language and literature are likewise little known so that the complex pattern of parody and allusion in Büchner's work is more an academic chore than the witty pastime it should be for the reader to pursue. Added to this is the specific wit of Büchner's Hessian dialect, full of nicknames, folk-lore, proverbs and slang which make the details of his writing hard of access even to the reader familiar with 'high' German. I have paid particular attention to the background against which Büchner wrote to make this access easier, matter which the reader new to Büchner may wish to leave out and return to later. Understanding Büchner is like scaling a high peak whose summit cannot be reached without hard work through the foothills. The reward is the view from the top.

Karl Georg Büchner was born on 17 October 1813 in Godelau, a little farming village on the Rhine's alluvial plain near Darmstadt. At that time Darmstadt was the capital of the Grand Duchy of Hessen-Darmstadt and is still an important administrative and cultural centre in the modern West German state of Hessen.[5] By an accident of history, Büchner was born in the same year as Richard Wagner and both men were involved in radical politics: one wonders if Büchner's left-wing views would have changed as radically as Wagner's! The house where he was born still stands, though no longer in the possession of the family, and a small plaque, high up on the wall facing the street, commemorates the event. His father Ernst and grandfather Jakob Karl were doctors and both Georg and his younger brother Ludwig followed the family tradition. Ludwig, in fact, became far more famous in his lifetime than Georg, through the widespread popularity of his treatise *Kraft und Stoff* which was translated into many languages.[6]

When Georg was three his father was appointed medical adviser to the Darmstadt court of Grand Duke Ludwig I and it was in Darmstadt that he grew up and went to school. His first teacher was his mother Caroline whose influence, argues Anton Büchner, was paramount in his life. She taught him to read and write and the rudiments of mathematics; she also introduced him to the new Romantic literature and above all to Schiller, her favourite. Her talents are evident from the fact that four of her children became successful authors and two celebrities in their lifetimes, Ludwig and Luise, whose novels and writings about women's rights became highly influential.

At nine Georg entered a private preparatory school and then in March 1825 he started at the Ludwig-Georg Gymnasium (High School) which he attended until Easter 1831. It was his interest in natural science coupled with great energy that distinguished his time as schoolboy, but as a number of surviving short works show, most notably the *Cato-speech*, his interest in philosophy was also well-developed. The key question for him was suicide and in *Cato* he passionately defends the right of the individual to decide about the length of his own life.

In her novel *Ein Dichter* (*A Poet*) Luise describes the world in which she and her brothers grew up and attacks 'the intellectual stagnation of small towns where a genius is treated like a fool and where talent either withers away or is systematically ground down, if it gets caught up in the magic circles where the very worst intellectual narrow-mindedness is king.'[7] This claustrophobic atmosphere was a major fact in Büchner's later political development. Later she portrays Georg, in the persona of Ludwig Brandeis, delivering his *Cato-speech*:

> Both the slim, willowy figure and the expression on his
> face had a girlish air to them, and the thin, white hands
> with which he pressed the paper to his chest in no way
> contradicted the impression. By contrast, the high,
> powerful forehead on which the soft waves of his chest-
> nut brown hair were curled. They spoke of the thinker
> and researcher to be, as did the gentle, infinitely graceful
> mouth and the poetic spirit. The eyes were grey and
> looked on occasion, by reason of their short-sighted-
> ness, flat and dull, an aspect reinforced by the dreaming
> brooding to which Ludwig happily abandoned himself.[8]

The novel is not complete, but it is clear that Luise thought
society to blame for her brother's death.

In the autumn of 1831, seemingly more to please his
father than from any strong personal conviction, Büchner
travelled to the University of Strasbourg for his first semes-
ter as medical student. Here he remained for two happy
years. He found lodgings at the house of Pastor Johann
Jakob Jaeglé, a widower, with whom his relatives in the city
were friendly. Jaeglé lived with his daughter Wilhelmine,
known affectionately as Minna, in the Rue St Guillaume.
Though three years Büchner's senior, Minna fell in love
with him and the pair were soon secretly engaged. She
never married.

As well as love, Strasbourg offered Büchner politics: no
other city in Europe at the time was quite so radical and tur-
bulent.[9] It had been a main centre outside Paris of the agitation that preceded the rise of Louis XVIII in the glorious
July days of 1830 and it was a favoured resort of German
exiles, in safety just the French side of the Rhine. Nowhere
was activity more concentrated than in the Medical Faculty
where Büchner was to study.

Perhaps this in itself would not have radicalised Büchner, but on 3 April 1833 an event occurred which seemed to crystallise his thought. A group of Frankfurt students and a handful of Polish nationalists tried, rather futilely, to storm the Frankfurt guardhouse. This putsch, as it became known, failed lamentably in its immediate object, but it drew from Büchner a significantly fiery response. On 5 April he wrote to his family:

> If anything can help in our time it is *violence*. [. . .] Young people are reproached for using violence. But aren't we in a permanent state of violence? Because we were born and bred in jail we don't notice any more that we are stuck in clink, with chains on our hands and feet and gags in our mouths. What do you call *a lawful state*? *A law* that turns the great mass of citizens into serf-like cattle in order to satisfy the unnatural needs of an insignificant and decayed minority? And this law, supported by brute military force and the stupid intrigues of its agents, this law is an *eternal cloddish force* attacking justice and sound reason and I will fight against it *verbally* and *physically* wherever I can.[10]

His anger is not without cause. Before the great European wars from 1792–1815, what we now know as Germany, both East and West, Austria, Hungary and parts of Poland, Russia, Czechoslovakia, Italy and Jugoslavia were part of a strange and disparate agglomeration of sovereign states, approximately six hundred in all, that were grouped under the title Holy Roman Empire. Many of these were still organised along the same sort of lines as in the Middle Ages which meant, for example, that the peasantry were treated as the private property of their rulers. When the Napoleonic armies swept across Europe this crumbling organisation totally collapsed: in its place Napoleon put a mere 38 states, redrawing boundaries to create more manageable administrative units. He introduced his *Code Napoleon* to change many legal practices and with his armies came both the more liberal French culture and, more important, a glimpse of democracy, however much Napoleon's own imperialist style repressed democratic tendencies. Suddenly merit not birth was the way to success, a fact which greatly influenced the career of Büchner's father.[11]

When peace came in 1815 much of what Napoleon had done was retained. The 38 rulers found it in their own interests to keep the boundaries they had been newly given and even much of the *Code* was kept. Lost however, was the democratic undertone to the French occupying presence and in its place grew more strongly than ever a new form of imperialist feudalism that had most of the faults and few of the virtues of Napoleon's administration. Privilege returned on a scale beyond that of pre-1789 and such achievements as had survived of the French Revolution seemed to have slipped through men's fingers.

This process of refeudalisation did not happen at a stroke but rather crept up on Germany in the ensuing decades through the agency of the Austrian Chancellor, Prince Metternich. Metternich had a 'System', as it became known, for controlling and eradicating political opposition consisting of measures all too familiar in our own times – secret police, press censorship and *agents provocateurs*. Repression began with the Karlsbad decrees of 1819 against the then newly-founded progressive nationalist student groups – the *Burschenschaften* – and by the 1830s the last vestiges of free expression were removed when both the *Pressverein* (the association of independent publishers) and the 'Young Germans' were banned.

Most of the middle classes from whom opposition could

have come stayed silent. Typical of these was Büchner's father, Ernst, who had transferred his enthusiasm for Napoleon to his Grand Duke and been well rewarded for doing so. Not unnaturally his son's letter worried him and in an exchange of notes he tried to steer him away from the dangerous waters of radicalism. But fate was against him: after two years in Strasbourg Büchner was required by Hessian university statute to complete his studies at a home university and that happened to be Giessen, the very place from where the Frankfurt putsch had been planned.

In the autumn of 1833 Büchner arrived in Giessen, but he was soon on his way home again, ill. The strain of parting from Minna, the dullness of Giessen after Strasbourg and the coldness he felt towards his new colleagues combined to depress him severely and he spent the time to Christmas recovering. Psychosomatic illness of this sort is not uncommon in writers – Goethe had a similar problem – but it does gloss his sister's description of his 'girlishness'. On returning to Giessen in the New Year he sought relief in radical reading and politics. He told Minna that March:

> I studied the history of the Revolution. I had the feeling of being annihilated by the atrocious fatalism of history. I find a heinous uniformity in human nature, an inescapable violence in human conditions, given to all and to none. The individual is merely foam on a wave, greatness mere accident, the rule of genius is puppetry, a ridiculous wrestling with an iron law in which the greatest achievement is simply to become aware of it, overcoming it is impossible.[12]

This passage and the development of its ideas in the rest of Büchner's work shows a marked affinity with the thinking of the young Karl Marx, as many have pointed out. But

Büchner did not, unlike Marx, lose faith in the individual as the core of the struggle for social change, giving the individual that importance which Marx ascribed to class.

Büchner was not all intellectual activist and his letters to Minna reveal a tenderness and sensuality not unlike those of Keats (with whom he has much in common) to Fanny Brawne:

> Can't you hear my steps returning again to you? Look, I send you kisses, snowdrops, primroses, violets, the soil's first timid glances into the flaming eye of the sun youth. Half the day I sit locked up with your picture and talk to you. Yesterday morning I promised you flowers; here they are. What will you give me in return? How do you like my Bedlam? When I want to do something serious I am like Larifari [Punch] in the comedy; when he goes to draw his sword he pulls only a rabbit's tail.[13]

The favoured puppet imagery here combines with an equally characteristic sensuality which is one of the key elements in all the plays.

Büchner's political concern soon brought him into the circle around the radical Giessen pastor, Ludwig Weidig, with whom he established a close if not always harmonious relationship.[14] Though an opponent of violence, Weidig knew in advance of the Frankfurt putsch and both he and his visitors were under surveillance. Like his English counterparts, Robert Owen and Elizabeth Gaskell, Weidig believed that God's will would be decisive in any moves for reform and that God would give the sign for action in His good time. While it was a Christian's duty to spread the gospel and agitate for improvement he should avoid the risk of direct confrontation with the state. Büchner the free-thinker disagreed, arguing that men should help them-

11

selves. It was not to heaven we should direct our thoughts but to earth. He accordingly set up the Giessen branch of the Society for the Rights of Man, a secret organisation he had first encountered in Strasbourg which was committed both to common ownership and violence. Its most distinctive feature was that it was prepared, as the academic *Burschenschaften* were not, to admit to its ranks radical apprentices and labourers and from contemporary court records we know that its activities were taken very seriously by its members and the authorities alike.

The result of this political activity was the *Hessian Peasant Courier* drafted early in 1834 with the help of statistical information assembled by Weidig. Stylistically the work is a compromise between Büchner's radical calls for action and Weidig's more temperate and Christian arguments for equity and brotherhood, but although Büchner did find Weidig's editing irksome (substituting *vornehm* – here meaning 'aristocratic' – for *reich* – 'rich') the result was neither the estrangement of the two as so often claimed, nor a significant dilution of its message. Politically the work achieved nothing, but, as a result of the presence in the Society of a police informer, Konrad Kuhl, it led to the gradual arrest of a number of its members. First to be caught was Büchner's closest friend, Karl Minnigerode, son of the then highest official in the Hessian Ministry of Justice, who had the misfortune to be in possession of copies of the pamphlet when the police picked him up. Büchner was known to be involved in some way, but for some reason Kuhl kept the details back; although Büchner's rooms were searched he was not arrested. Denying all involvement to his family he returned to Darmstadt for the summer to be kept under close surveillance by his suspicious father.

In charge of investigating the case was the examining

magistrate Georgi whom Büchner first encountered at Giessen, laughing, a little hysterically, at the man's slowness. Georgi was a vindictive alcoholic who managed in due course to break the will of Minnigerode and another member of the society, Gustav Clemm, who confessed under torture. Later still he drove Weidig to suicide. He and his police were, according to Büchner, the muses of *Danton's Death*.[15]

While there is no final explanation of the creative surge which began with *Danton*, four factors did coalesce in Büchner's mind at the turn of 1834 and 1835: fear of arrest and torture, affinity with Georges Danton, hero of the French Revolution, his need for money to escape from Darmstadt and a sudden personal experience of that 'fatalism of history' in the form both of Georgi and of his father, who had effectively become his jailer. Behind all these lay sheer disappointment at the failure of the *Courier*. Rather naively, Büchner had probably hoped that his pamphlet would bring the masses out in revolt, like Danton's oratory. He need not have been ashamed at the pamphlet, but Hessen in 1834 was not Paris in 1789.

There was perhaps one more factor at work, more artistic than political and not unmixed with ambition. The young Schiller, his mother's idol, had shot to fame at little over twenty with his first play *The Robbers* which, among other things, took the despotism of his Prince, Karl Eugen of Württemberg, to task. When Büchner set about *Danton* similar thoughts may well have crossed his mind. Could he make himself a nationally known figure with his pen? Büchner was not averse to self-dramatisation and in the letter he sent to Karl Gutzkow with his finished manuscript of the play there are too many references to Schiller's robber hero, Karl von Moor, to be overlooked:

Georg Büchner

Dear Sir,

Perhaps your own observation, or, in less happy circumstances, perhaps your own experience will have informed you that there is a degree of misery that forgets any sense of tact and silences, any feeling of delicacy. There are of course, people who say that in such a situation one should rather starve one-self out of the world, but I could in rejection of this view, offer the reply of the recently blinded Captain from the back-street who said he would shoot himself were he not bound to support his family by staying alive to receive his pension. That is terrible. You will certainly agree then that there can be similar circumstances that prevent one from making one's body into a sheet-anchor and throwing it from the wreck of this world into the water, and will not therefore be surprised that I break open your door, enter your study, press a manuscript to your breast and beg for alms. [. . .]

About the work itself there is very little more that I can say than that difficult circumstances forced me to write it in a maximum of five weeks. I tell you this to sway your judgement of the author, not of his play as such. What I should do with it I do not myself know; I know only that I have every reason to blush in the sight of history: yet I comfort myself with the thought that, with the exception of Shakespeare, every poet stands before history and before nature like a schoolboy. [. . .]

Should the tone of this letter perhaps alienate you, please consider that I find it easier to beg in rags than hand over a supplication dressed in a frock coat, and almost easier to say, a pistol in my hand, 'La bourse ou la vie' than with trembling lips to whisper 'May God reward you'.[16]

This last paragraph is the language of Karl von Moor, but neither it, nor the poise with which he writes, can disguise his exhaustion. Gutzkow did as he was asked, took the play that night to the publisher Sauerländer, who agreed to publish it. As however, the original version would have meant the certain closure of Sauerländer's press he and Gutzkow agreed to consult with Büchner on toning it down. The process took too long to be of use to his escape plan, but Büchner very likely had access to secret funds of his Society to help him in emergency: on 9 March Büchner crossed into France without a passport.

His letter of the same day reveals how the decision troubled him:

> Don't you worry at all about my personal safety. [. . .] Only the most pressing reasons forced me to leave my fatherland and my father's house in this way. . . . I could have surrendered to the inquisition. I had nothing to fear of the outcome of the investigation but everything of the investigation itself. [. . .] I would have been set free, but left a physical and spiritual wreck. [. . .] Now my hands and my head are free . . . . Now everything is up to me. I shall pursue my medico-philosophical studies with every effort, and there is still room enough in *that* field to achieve something substantial, for our age is so constituted as to value such work.[17]

Büchner knew he was not the stuff of which political martyrs are made, but he is not strictly honest when he says he had nothing to fear of the outcome of the investigation since he was the main instigator of the whole affair. This does raise a difficult problem: was Büchner right to leave at a time when his friend Minnigerode was suffering effectively on his behalf? Is Büchner to be seen as a traitor to his friend? The question is easier to ask than to answer, both morally and politically. German history is alas more than most a history of sending writers into exile or forcing them to suicide. Heine, Marx and Büchner, Benjamin, Brecht, Tucholsky, Hasenclever and Mann are just a few who have suffered this way in the past two centuries. What should Büchner have done? Giving himself up would certainly not have helped Minnigerode. Nevertheless, fear of arrest and a deep sense of having betrayed his friend did dog him till his death and his final fever fantasies were full of such thoughts.

Danton, published in mid-1835, was not a great success with the public, but Gutzkow knew that here was a major new writer. For Büchner the act of writing was cathartic, shedding the strain of the months of waiting, but shedding too some of the young man's mannerisms. His letters thereafter sounded a profounder note. From his Strasbourg exile a new role begins to emerge for him in a distinctly classical tradition, that of the artist as doctor to the diseases of a sick society. In this way his two principal talents reached a highly productive symbiotic relationship, the dramatic writing gaining the objective precision of the medical research and the medical research winning the social commitment and energy of the drama.

The results were spectacular: in the period March 1835 to October 1836, in exile, he wrote *Lenz* and the first draft of *Woyzeck*, – both of which have a strong medical component – *Leonce and Lena*, his doctoral thesis *On the Nervous System of the Barbel* and inaugural lecture *On the Nerves of the Skull*, and his philosophical essays, and translated two of Victor Hugo's plays. But Büchner was, for all the success, restless and thinking hard about giving up medicine. In June 1836 Gutzkow in a warm and friendly letter warns against it.

My dear friend, you send me a sign you are alive and you
want one from me. [. . .] You seem to want to abandon
the art of medicine, a step which, so I hear, will not make
your father very pleased. Do not be so unfair on this dis-
cipline, since, or so it seems to me, you have it to thank
for your particular strength, by which I mean your
unusual lack of inhibition, your autopsy I almost want to
say, that comes across in everything you write. If you
join the ranks of German philosophers with this direct-
ness it is bound to cause a new movement.[18]

Gutzkow deserved his high reputation as a critic, and was
himself at the time of writing suffering heavily from the ban
on his and other 'Young German' writers' work, which
makes his warmth all the more generous.[19] Perhaps
Büchner listened: three months later he was on the way to
Zürich as Reader in Anatomy.

In retrospect his arrival in Zürich is like the apogee in the
turning of Büchner's wheel of fortune. Soon after settling in
he received news that led him to believe Minnigerode was
dead. His reaction, as his letter shows, was a vain attempt
to be calm:

Don't you worry about political activities here. Take no
notice of the old wives' tales in our newspapers. Switzerland is a republic [. . .] Here the streets are not full of
soldiers, probationer lawyers and lazy civil servants; one
does not risk being run down by an aristocratic coach;
instead one finds a healthy and strong people everywhere and for a little money a simple, good, purely
republican government, maintained through a *property
tax*, a kind of tax that in Germany would be decried as
the apogee of anarchy. [. . .]

Minnigerode is dead they tell me; that is, he was being

tortured to death for three years. Three years! The French butchers got you done in a few hours, first the judgement, then the guillotine. But three years! What a humane government we have, they can't stand blood.[20]

Switzerland is so significant because it proves that there is a form of government which can solve the 'bread' question – how to make adequate social provision for the whole population – and knowing this makes Büchner's rage and frustration all the greater that in Hessen nothing is being done. But he is also deeply shocked and his sense of himself as a traitor to his friend must have surfaced in his mind. Once before, in Giessen, he had been ill for seemingly psychosomatic reasons and surely shock was a factor in his low resistance to the fever he was soon to catch.

Büchner seems to have caught typhus, a disease even then rarely fatal to the fit and young. On 20 January 1837 he wrote brightly to Minna:

> I have caught cold and am lying in bed. But I am feeling better now. [. . .] Tomorrow I shall be back at my old trot, you won't believe how regular and orderly. I tick almost as reliably as a Black Forest clock. But this is good for me: after all that excited intellectual life to have peace and enjoy creative writing again. Poor Shakespeare was a copyist by day and had to write at night, and I, who am not worthy of untying his shoe laces, am so much better off. . .[21]

The unintentional irony of the last remark is brutal in retrospect. His letter reminds us again of the power Shakespeare had over him, and reveals how, at least in Zürich, creative writing was a relaxation for him.

By 14 February the illness was so bad that Minna was sent for and she arrived in one of his last short clear moments. On Sunday 19 February 1837, a bright sunny day, Georg Büchner died, aged twenty-three. He was buried shortly afterwards and a large congregation, including the mayor, attended his funeral.

Not least in his dying words is Büchner a mystery: from the notebook of Caroline Schulz, the friend who nursed him in his last three weeks, we learn that they were delivered in a clear voice and with no apparent trace of fever: 'We can never have too much pain, we can only have too little. Through pain we come to God!' – 'We are death, dust, ashes, how can we complain?'[22]

Was this truly a death-bed conversion? Or did he understand by God a projection of all that he wanted to be and was not? Was it perhaps another hallucination? Or was he worried about Minnigerode? There is nothing to suggest that Büchner was contemplating a return to the church, and indeed *Woyzeck* implies rather the opposite, but no one can predict his own reaction to imminent death.

Büchner's brief life was rich in what Keats terms 'negative capability' and his dying words exemplify the pleasure and the difficulty any writer has in fixing Georg Büchner in print. There are so many explanations, most of which are plausible, for his life and work and yet ultimately they are all part of a complex natural truth which is no more or less than that life and work itself. Nor is this sophistry: Büchner refused neat systems of explanation of the world he saw, and the worst insult to his memory would be to attempt in his name what he so strenuously denied.

2
A Man Out of His Time

The taste of the theatre-going public during the 1830s and the dramatic traditions on which Büchner drew are the subject of my next chapter, but to understand them their intellectual context needs first to be described here. When one relates Büchner's non-dramatic works to the central preoccupations of his time one sees how very closely Büchner both understood and contributed to defining the spirit of his age. Three issues stand out: the nature and purpose of the state; the nature and rights of the individual within that state; and the debate between science and religion as to how best to explain the world. Büchner had major statements to make on all three.

First the state. The most influential thinker of the age in the German-speaking world was G. W. F. Hegel (1770–1831)[1] for whom 'the laws and the constitution are the fundament [of the state], to which the individuals' highest duty is to submit their wills.' There is no contradiction between religion and this duty to the state, because the state is itself the highest expression of God's will on earth. Obedience to the state, therefore, is obedience to God. The origins of this thinking lie in Immanuel Kant's thesis, formulated in 1784 as 'The idea of a general history from the point of view of a citizen of the world'. In this work Kant poses one basic question: 'how is it possible that in the apparent freedom of the impulses of the will and actions of the individual human being that nevertheless seen as a whole there is a regular movement to world history?' The answer is quite simply: 'through the state this is possible.' Hegel develops this answer from what in Kant's hands is presented as an empirically observed fact into the manifestation of the reasonable and necessary working of the 'World Spirit'. History is thus defined as 'the reasonable, necessary movement of the World Spirit'.[2] This World Spirit is of its nature free, has its substance in itself, is independent, and exists for itself. Its purpose lies in the unfolding of itself in the life of the world, towards greater and greater freedom and ever-increasing reason. This process is not to be understood in a scientific or Darwinistic sense, where the central proposition is of an expedient view of progress caused by the evolution of better and more successful species, but rather as the revelation of a pre-determined plan. 'History' is thus the revelation of the plan through time; and although physical nature does have a minor role to play in the progress of history, it is, according to Hegel, the history of the intellect which really matters.[3]

Büchner's response to this perception of the state as agent of an historical plan is seemingly contradictory. He asks whether the natural struggle to eat and survive is not the true determinant of world history, at least as seen through the eyes of the 95 per cent of the world's population to whom the 'bread' question *is* history – a question which implicitly challenges the primacy of the institutions of the man-made state. But he also accepts the Hegelian

concept of inevitability, substituting 'natural law' for
'World Spirit' as the controlling force. Put in terms we shall
encounter in the plays, Büchner does not deny the immanent dynamic of history, but he locates it in nature not in the
city.

The resolution of the contradiction lies in that aspect of
Hegel's thought which his highly-placed pupils tended to
suppress, the statement that 'the history of the world is progress in the consciousness of freedom'.[4] What the average
German state singularly lacked in the 1830s was such freedom. The Hegelians could answer such a charge by claim-
ing that what Hegel meant was freedom of the spirit not
that of the tongue or body, but both Büchner and Karl
Marx rightly asked what the value was of such a consciousness of freedom if it were not to be converted into action.
Since 1815, they argued, Europe had gone backwards from
the triumphs of the French Revolution towards class privilege on a scale little dreamed of even before the Revolution. This retrogression, justified by reference to Hegel's
statements about obedience to the state, actually contra-
dicted his overall view of the inevitability of progress and
the essentially forward-moving nature of historical *dialectic*. To erect in Hegel's name a rigid and reactionary state
was an intellectual sham.[5]

Where Büchner diverges markedly from Hegel is in the
direction and purpose of the dialectic. Hegel is careful to
avoid any suggestion that progress means increased happiness: 'The idea pays the tribute of existence and of transi-
toriness not from itself but from the passions of individuals'.[6] Thus it comes about that at critical moments in history a leader or 'World Historical Individual' appears who
takes on the role of managing director of history, much as
Julius Caesar, Napoleon or Georges Danton had done.[7] As
soon as his role is fulfilled history casts him off like chaff

from the threshed wheat. Büchner, by contrast, equates progress with freedom, brotherhood, equity and the pursuit of happiness in the manner enshrined in the constitution of the United States of America. If the *dialectic* is to have any value it is in expressing the inevitability of the eventual solution of the 'bread' question. In other words, when it comes to the rights of the individual Büchner places them above those of the state, Hegel below.

Hegel's reasons for asserting the primacy of the state are good: it must mediate both between the conflicts of individual wills and between those collective wills and the World Spirit. Without the willing consent of the individual in the decisions of state, and thereby of God's will, history cannot progress: 'Only this view can make the Spirit come to terms with world history and reality, that all that has happened and happens every day could not only not happen without God, but essentially reveals the work of his own self'.[8] Such idealised pessimism, such ready acceptance that what is is, and is for the best, can easily be used to justify taking no action for reform. Reform, it is argued, will come when God wants it and until then we must accept things as they are. That this in practice means luxury for the few and penury for the many is, for Hegel, beside the point: but for Büchner it is the point. Whatever Hegel might himself believe, his pupils and followers are perpetrating such injustice in his name that the philosophy on which they rest their claims cannot at root be an equable one. In a world where man has no say in what happens will he not quite naturally drift into epicureanism, pursuit of sensation for its own sake and neglect what is his Christian or simply human duty to improve the lot of the starving? The question is at the heart of the *Courier*.

In privately distributing the *Courier* Büchner was adopting a well-tried method of circumventing the strict censorship in force since the banning of the *Pressverein* in 1832. This organisation had been the last to survive in the name of freedom of expression and its enforced closure meant the end of any open dialogue on political matters until the 'System' collapsed in 1848. Pamphleteering and underground presses became widespread but the penalties for such activity were high. Büchner knew that he was taking a big risk with the *Courier* but his hatred of privilege overturned any private doubts he may have entertained.

His chief target is the totalitarian aspect of the Hegelian state, and he asks bluntly who and what that state should be for: by what right do the few govern the many. Taking his motto from Tom Paine, the American revolutionary hero, he writes:

> Peace to the cottages! War to the palaces!
>
> In the year 1834 it looks as if the Bible was proved wrong. It looks as if God created the peasants and the artisans on the fifth day and the Princes and aristocrats on the sixth; and as if the Lord had told the latter 'Rule over the animals that crawl upon the earth' and it was as if he had numbered the peasants and citizens with the worms. [. . .]
>
> In the Grand Duchy of Hessen there are 718,373 inhabitants; they pay 6,363,364 guilders in taxes per year to the state. . . . This money is a blood tithe, drawn from the body of the people. [. . .]
>
> What is, then, that powerful thing, the state? [. . .] The state is everyone; the regulating forces of the state are the laws, which are there to protect the well-being of everyone. [. . .]
>
> Raise your eyes and count the handful of oppressors who are only strong through the blood they drain from you and from the arms you willingly hold out for them. There are about 10,000 of them in the Grand Duchy of

Hessen and about 700,000 of you and the ratio of oppres-
sors to people is the same in other German states. They
may well threaten with their armour and the King's
dragoons. But I tell you: he who raises the sword against
the people will die by the sword of the people. Germany
is now a field of corpses, soon it will be a paradise. The
German people is one body, you are a limb of this body.[9]

One misconception it is important to dispel is that the
Courier was isolated in identifying the extreme crisis of con-
fidence into which the 'System' was slipping. This was well
known. In Hessen, for example, a report was presented to
the court at Speyer in which reference is made to 'a state of
war between the rich and the poor'.[10] There can, however,
be no denying the exceptionally strong tone of Büchner's
writing, its explicit call for German unity and its acceptance
of violence as a means to that end, all propositions which
can be traced back to principles enshrined in the manifesto
of the French Revolution, *The Declaration of the Rights of
Man and of the Citizen* (1793), which Büchner had recently
been reading. This by its very title contradicts the Hegelian
thesis that the state has the supreme right,[11] and when
Büchner encourages the peasant to rise he is resting his case
on its last article which states: 'When the government
violates the rights of the people, rebellion is for the people
as a whole, and for all sections of the people the most sacred
and most pressing of their duties.' This, allowing for Weidig's christianising editing, is paraphrased by Büchner in
his closing rallying cry:

When the Lord signifies to you the men through whom
he shall lead the people out of bondage to freedom, you
shall rise and the whole body shall rise with you.[12]

The view of the state as a body is an old image, at first sight
suggestive of a possible compromise between the Hegelian

state and revolutionary democracy: but when one refers back to the statement 'The state is everyone . . . the laws . . . are there to protect the well-being of everyone' the possibility is soon dispelled.

Seen in the context of the rest of his thinking about history the most distinctively Büchnerian image in the *Courier* concerns the 'puppet-show' of history:

> If an honest man enters a council of state he is thrown out. But even if an honest man were at present or could remain a minister, he would be, as things stand in Germany, only a puppet on wires, on which a princely puppet pulls and on the princely bugbear pulls in turn his wife and her favourite or his half-brother or a gentleman-in-waiting or a coachman – or all together.[13]

The puppet is caught in a vertiginous prospect of puppets working puppets working puppets, no one knowing who is truly puppeteer and everyone suffering. The image attacks the Hegelian Spirit as just such an unseen puppeteer and asks, in the context of the actual state of affairs in Hessen, whether a good God could seriously will such things to happen. If so, is it not our duty to try to emancipate ourselves from Him? In other words, whatever its real purpose was intended to be, Hegelian thought has become a weapon in the hands of the mighty in their war with the weak.

In exile in France, the direct result of writing this pamphlet, the full weight of the contradictions in the present function of the German state led Büchner towards a different aspect of its malignity: its treatment of the exceptional individual. As well as providing bread, shelter and education for all its citizens, the advanced state should be in a position to foster special talents. But Büchner saw both in his own predicament and in the madness of the poet Lenz classic examples of the grinding monotony of rigid systems of government causing the alienation or exclusion of the gifted individual from society. The result of his engagement with this issue was what some consider his finest work, *Lenz*, a fragment of a novel that, in my own view, was deliberately fragmentary and must be regarded as 'complete' in its extant form.

Jakob Michael Reinhold Lenz (1751–1792) was perhaps the most talented of all the *Sturm und Drang* writers, a playwright, poet and essayist of great gifts though with a pathological inability to maintain his initial creative impulse through to a conclusion. Not unlike Samuel Johnson's friend Richard Savage, mental illness increasingly debilitated him and when he died in a Moscow gutter he had more or less been forgotten. Büchner was drawn to him initially through reading the diary of Pastor Oberlin with whom Lenz stayed in the early phase of his illness. In this work Oberlin describes with great care the difficulties he had with Lenz and yet also captures the thrilling brilliance of the man in his clearer moments. When Oberlin died his papers passed into the hands of Pastor Jaeglé, Büchner's father-in-law to be, who gave them to Büchner. As Büchner read, he saw how close the affinity was between himself and Lenz, their shared love for Shakespeare, their allied perceptions of nature and their common experience of emotional disorientation which, at the time, was uppermost in Büchner's mind.

Lenz travelled to stay with Oberlin in the hope that life in Oberlin's parish in the Vosges mountains would, through its closeness to nature, restore the balance of his mind. Büchner accordingly first shows him moving rapidly over the mountains, wishing all the time that he could move still quicker. Lenz's 'time' is evidently out of step with nature's:

Everything was so small to him, so close, so wet, he wished he could warm the earth behind the stove, he did not understand that he would need so much time to climb down a steep slope and get to a far distant point; he thought everything must be attainable in a few steps.[14]

The Oedipal relationship between Büchner and his subject is evident from the outset, as are two levels on which the discourse works – the personal and the socio-political. Lenz is disorientated and in conflict with his environment: but so is Büchner, the radical activist. He hoped to reach a far-distant point in a few steps – the liberation of the Hessian peasant – a course which he now must learn takes time. He hopes, like Lenz, that understanding nature will enable him to work more effectively, but while Lenz is concerned solely with his own psychological balance Büchner is pursuing the cause of the underprivileged.

The first step for both men is to come to terms with their struggles, with the great storms raging within them:

... he thought he must draw the storm into himself, take hold of everything in himself, he stretched himself out and lay on the earth, he burrowed himself into the universe, it was a desire that gave him pain.[15]

Lenz's thought patterns, with their echoes of *King Lear*, and his erratic actions are consciously reflected by Büchner in an exploded sentence structure, one descriptive unit, one sense-impression following another with no attempt by the author to impose on the information thus conveyed a syntactical order or even hierarchy of explanation or comment. Rather, by the use of clauses suspended in a form of apposition to one another a specific state of mind is conveyed, a quality of experience. Significantly, not just Lenz but Danton, Leonce and Woyzeck all lie down on the earth at the critical juncture of their lives, all trying to work out through contact with the earth their own sense of space and time. At times, all four worry that the sky is going to suffocate them: at times, they ride the cosmos like a horse. But all in moments of stress abandon formal syntax in favour of what we now call 'stream of consciousness', a technique Büchner may even be held to have invented.

The abandonment of formal syntax is indicative of a lack of moral order in the cosmos: there is only being in its most immediate form. What draws Lenz to Oberlin is that Oberlin, though a 'civilised' man, has the force of 'uncivilised' (but not brutish) being or nature in his eyes and face:

> Everything worked beneficially and soothingly on him, he felt compelled to look often into Oberlin's eyes and the powerful stillness that overcomes us in nature at rest, in the deep wood in the moonlit, melting summer nights, seemed to him nearer still in this quiet eye, this noble, earnest face.[16]

In one of the moments when Lenz has regained his composure he develops this theme further:

> The simplest, purest nature is closest bound to the elemental and the finer a man feels and lives intellectually, the duller will this elemental sense become.[17]

The riposte to Hegel is quite explicit, and to reinforce the point Lenz then goes on to instance two writers and one type of 'literature' who have both the quality of great art, and the elemental power of nature within them. These are Shakespeare, Goethe and the folk-song: the rest, says

29

Lenz, can be burned.[18] Neither Lenz nor Büchner had any time for trite and whimsical ideologies, a point on which he felt himself at variance with Gutzkow and the 'Young Germans' whom Gutzkow was gathering around him for his new *Review*. This is made very clear by Lenz in what is his last lucid speech:

> [Lenz] said: the poets of whom it is said that they offer reality had no idea what reality is, but at least they were better than those who wish to transfigure it. He said: the Good Lord has made the world as it should be and we cannot knock up anything to better it, so our sole aim should be to do a little in the way of following his example. In summary, I demand – life, the possibility of existence, and that's enough; we are not then required to ask if a thing is beautiful or if it is ugly, the feeling that something has been created stands above either of these and is the only criterion in artistic achievement.[19]

Almost identical sentiments can be found in Büchner's letters and from them it is clear that the desire for 'life' as described here is not a modish pursuit of literalism but rather a wish to penetrate the essence of what is described. This process, as we shall see in the plays, is essentially metaphoric, inclusive of politics but not necessarily political and one whose creative energy is drawn from love: each man is worthy of love and cannot be understood if unloved. Oberlin's concern for Lenz is offered as an example of such love and he becomes as much the protagonist of *Lenz* as the central figure himself.

While Büchner penetrates Lenz's mind to a degree that his words and Lenz's become indistinguishable, he also, as Lehmann's edition of the parallel texts of *Lenz* and Oberlin's Diary shows,[20] observed the schizophrenic condition with an accuracy hitherto unknown in medical writing. Büchner is able to balance complete involvement with his subject with complete detachment, a technique he also uses in the plays where the protagonist is used both as central consciousness and chorus. *Lenz* bridges the playwright and the scientist in Büchner, presenting in language comprehensible to the average, but intelligent, reader the explanation of a particular human condition on a personal, literary, sociological and scientific level. Metaphor is the means by which the discourse can successfully contain all four at once and at the same time suggest their congruence, a perception that far transcends any tendentious purpose and attempts a construction of a new philosophy of exact scientific investigation combined with love for what is observed.

In attempting a solution to the debate between religion and science in this manner, Büchner was drawing on his readings of Descartes and Spinoza, both of whom dealt with the problem in great detail. His vision of man's place in nature is distinctly Cartesian, the co-ordinates on which man is located being variously describable as 'Scientific' and 'Philosophical', 'Intellectual' and 'Natural', 'Literal' and 'Metaphoric', 'Physiological' and 'Sociological'. But, for Büchner, what determines and animates the grid on which these co-ordinates may be located was the fact and love of existence in itself, independent of any morality or divine plan, justifying itself by its being. He criticises Descartes for looking to God for explanations in an image that contrasts strangely with the otherwise sober tone of the Cartesius essay:

It is God who fills the gulf between thought and perception, between subject and object. He is the bridge between *cogito ergo sum*, between the lone, perplexed, single being, self-awareness, certain thought and the

31

outer world. The attempt is somewhat naive in execution but one sees nevertheless how instinctively precise is Cartesius's measurement of the grave of philosophy; and it is certainly strange how he uses the Good Lord as a ladder to crawl out of it.[21]

This image of philosophy as a grave, and the determined refusal to use God as a prop to man's weak spirit, is one that underlies all three plays. Its weakness is that it is negative: Büchner does not say what we must do. What of the positive side? The answer here is nature, and nature as defined in terms drawn from Büchner's critique of Spinoza.

In a scene in *Danton* that has very little to do with the rest of the play Tom Paine and Chaumette are talking about atheism as the ultimate step of rational man in his pursuit of liberation from religion and superstition:

PAINE: Remove all imperfection; only then can you demonstrate God; Spinoza has tried it. You can deny evil but not pain: only reason can prove God, but feeling raises itself against him. Consider this, Anaxagoras, why do I suffer? That is the sheer cliff of atheism. The smallest twitch of pain, and that only in a single atom, sends a crack through creation from top to bottom.[22]

In this speech one historical rather than metaphorical congruence between Büchner's literary, scientific and philosophical writing is suggested: suffering. The duty of the writer, the doctor and the thinker is to diagnose the cause of suffering and alleviate or cure it. This is the thread that links *Lenz*, the *Courier* and Büchner's philosophy. And what is the first step towards cure? Ridding oneself of the need for God:

PAINE: First you prove God from morality and then morality from God. What do you want from your morality? I do not know if there is in itself anything good or bad and have therefore no cause to alter my behaviour accordingly. I act as my nature tells me I should, what is suitable for it is suitable for me and what is unsuitable is bad and so I don't do it and protect myself from it when it comes in my direction.[23]

The words are not the historical Paine's but Büchner's. In them the essential primacy of nature is unmistakable, a primacy whose acceptance brings the emancipation of the individual. From that emancipation, so argued Büchner, all else follows. It would be wrong to see this as a radically new idea, however radical Büchner's personal emphasis on it was. The pursuit of liberty and individual happiness was an ideal that went hand-in-glove with the development of German theatrical writing from its renaissance in Lessing's hands through to Büchner and beyond; this renaissance and its contribution to the climate in which the playwright Büchner wrote I shall now examine.

3
A Tradition of Dissent

Büchner's concern for the individual's position in the state is central to all his work: but whereas in the *Courier* he deals with the immediate problems of Hessian politics in the 1830s, he uses the plays to explore the question in a more general and long-term manner. When he died his views were, however, still forming: much of his extant work is fragmentary or obscure. While I cannot pretend to illuminate all these obscurities a good many can be understood by reference to what Büchner had read and the tradition in which he stood as a dramatist. This tradition was one of dissent.

Four issues had claimed the attention of serious German dramatists since the mid-eighteenth century: their attempt to free their art from the restrictive rules of French neo-classicism and to create their own native theatrical mode; their concern for the non-aristocratic individual and his state of mind; their pursuit of educational goals through theatre; and their view of the theatre as an organ of dissent in the body politic. The most significant effect of their work was that it attracted political as well as cultural opposition, largely because they framed their aesthetic demands with a plea for freedom of a political kind. Lessing, Lenz, Schiller, Goethe, Tieck and Grabbe all wanted freedom and their efforts to achieve it constitute the most remarkable century so far in German theatre. Büchner stands at the end of this movement, drawing from it its admiration for Shakespeare, *the* genius, an admiration that dwarfed his feelings for any other writer. He was, like his predecessors, well-educated and widely read. He knew Latin and French fluently and could read Italian and possibly English. He was an intellectual who delighted in allusion and concealed meaning. Even at his most artless he belongs to a sophisticated mode of writing.

Büchner's closeness to the dissenters is clear from his choice of central figures in his plays. Danton is a revolutionary at the end of his political career whom Büchner uses to explore the nature of the revolutionary mind. Leonce is a prince, about to become King, who is exposed to feelings and political issues in an educational series of encounters. Woyzeck is an alienated misfit who tries in vain to understand the society that has rejected him. All three approach the problem of the individual's place in society and all three deal with special, yet typical individuals.

This may not now seem very radical, but it was in the 1830s, particularly from a man in political exile. To understand Büchner's commitment to this tradition of literary and dramatic radicalism is not only to confront the more overtly political aspects of his plays but also to recognise even in his more covert references – notably in *Leonce and Lena* – a consistently dissenting stance. This means that the 'texts' of his plays can only be understood in relationship to those other 'texts' to which they refer or allude. I have space for only a small selection of these, but all deal with one or more of the four issues I describe above. I do not think it possible to approach Büchner without some visit to what André Malraux would call his 'imaginary museum'.

Lessing, Father of the Dissenting Tradition

Gotthold Ephraim Lessing (1729–81),[1] dramatist, dramaturg, essayist, satirist, polemicist, theologian, librarian, citizen of the world and noble soul marks the end of a period of sterility in German literature, especially dramatic, which goes back perhaps as far as Hans Sachs in sixteenth-century Nürnberg. Through Lessing Shakespeare in the original form was introduced to Germany and the lessons of Shakespearian theatre applied to German. Plagued by financial and political problems Lessing never achieved the security of Goethe in Weimar, but it is unlikely Goethe could have enjoyed that security without the gifts to German letters selflessly bestowed by Lessing. Apart from Shakespeare, these were two-fold, the use of bourgeois plots in tragedy and a vocabulary of opposition to French neo-classical rules.

Shakespeare was doubly important to Lessing: he was the greatest playwright he had read, a man whose insight into human nature was the best possible education into the world of feeling; and Shakespeare offered him the practical example he needed to liberate German theatre from the bondage of the French, the neo-classical unities of the tragedies of Racine and Corneille. Using Shakespeare as shield, Lessing fought the French on two fronts, the practical and the theoretical.

In his famous collection of essays, the so-called *Hamburg Dramaturgy* (1767–69) he initiated a theoretical alternative to neo-classicism with the aim of proving 'Even with the example of the ancients as the basis for comparison Shakespeare is a far greater tragic poet than Corneille.'[2] While such a case seems less than revolutionary today, it brought Lessing into disfavour with both the aesthetic and the political establishment, an experience Büchner too was to face. In direct terms this meant conflict with the doyen of German neo-classicism Johann Christoph Gottsched (1700–66). Gottsched published what amounted to a set of rules for playwrights to observe in writing for the stage, *Attempt at a Critical Art of Poetry* (1730), which was very influential. Its rules were six-fold: the poet must adopt a moral theme; he should devise a plot-structure that will allow him to develop this theme and illustrate it; he should then search history for an example of the moral, history being safer than the poet's own imagination; he should tailor the history to suit the moral; he should divide the work into five equal acts; and finally he should rework his plot into lofty, metrical couplets to suit the high tone of his argument. Of course, *en passant*, the unities of place, time and action would be observed.

Lessing, borrowing that favourite Augustan term, dubbed Gottsched a 'dunce': Gottsched should know, he wrote 'that we take more after the taste of the English than the French; that we want to see and think more in our tragedies than in French tragedy is to be seen or thought; that the great, the terrible, the melancholic achieves greater effect on us than the clever, the tender, the amorous; that too much simplicity tires us more than too much complication.'[3] Our sympathies now undoubtedly lie with Lessing, but he had a target in Gottsched not unworthy of his attack.

Lessing attracted Gottsched's anger at first not for his theory but for his practice; in 1755 he had written the first bourgeois tragedy in the German language, and as such the first 'modern' German play. This was *Miss Sara Sampson*, a work whose plot drew heavily both on Congreve's *The Double Dealer*, – even taking over names like Mellefont – and on Richardson's *Clarissa*. As well as proving Gottsched wrong in practice – the audience's reaction was immensely enthusiastic and full of praise at the play's realism and psychological insight – Lessing also opened up a dialogue between novelistic and dramatic modes of writing. This had two decisive benefits: in the confrontation between Sara herself and her rival Marwood, Lessing showed that simple, colloquial prose could be every bit as powerful as high verse in conveying a tragic situation; he also demonstrated that tragedy is the property of a tragic situation, not of the sufferings of the upper class. The lesson was not lost on Büchner, especially in *Woyzeck* and *Lenz*.

With his next play, *Minna von Barnhelm* (1767), Lessing opened up two other issues which were to be of importance to Büchner: the cause of German unity and the function of theatre in politics. The precise concern of *Minna* was the antagonism between Prussia and Saxony, which not only kept weakening both states, but caused debilitating personal suffering. This brought him to reiterate the implication of *Sara Sampson* that every man has tragic potential:

> The names of Princes and heros can add pomp and majesty to a play: but they contribute nothing towards its emotion. The misfortune of those whose conditions are most like our own must, quite naturally, go deepest into our souls; and if we have sympathy with kings it is with them as men and not as kings. If their class makes their misfortunes more important it does not make them more interesting. It may be that whole peoples are bound up with them: but our sympathies require a single object and a state is far too abstract a concept for our perception.[4]

Long before Hegel, and long before Metternich's 'System' Lessing was developing a language of opposition for the German intellectual.

Goethe recognised the nature and extent of the achievement:

> The first themes that were truly drawn from life and yet of really more lasting importance entered German poetry through the reign of Frederick the Great and the Seven Years' War. [. . .] Here I must above all mention with honour one work, the most truthful product of the Seven Years' War and of perfectly north German national content. It is the first theatre production drawn from significant life of specifically contemporary content, which for that very reason had an impact that is incalculable: *Minna von Barnhelm*.[5]

Into this select and influential category of plays whose contemporary specificity have general importance fit all of Büchner's and there is no doubt that Lessing, in initiating such a dramatic style, substantially defined the literary stance which brought out the best in Büchner.

Lenz: the Attack on Aristotle

Lenz's influence on Büchner was considerable – this we have seen in *Lenz* – but it extended into Büchner's stage work as well. Lenz was a highly innovative playwright. Lenz's idol was Shakespeare whom he translated, imitated and wrote about in the manner Lessing had initiated. This made his work especially fertile for Büchner, who found in it themes, images and structural techniques which he could use, as well as a sensitive understanding of Shakespeare's genius.

Lenz's two best known plays, *The Soldiers* (1776) and *The Private Tutor* (1774), both carry the generic designation 'comedy' but are no more comic than *Leonce and Lena*. In both, pressing themes of the day are debated, the Prussian law against soldiers marrying, which was turning garrison towns into disaster areas for susceptible girls and giving soldiers unlimited licence in their sexual activity, and the miserable treatment of the private tutor in a decadent educational system favouring only the rich and privileged. In both plays there is close examination of the conflict between the generations which adds a broader sociological dimension to Lenz's immediate political concerns. The general appeal of such a politically engaged attitude to character to Büchner, as indeed later to Brecht, is obvious, and feeds directly into characters like Danton and Woyzeck. More specifically, Lenz showed Büchner how to organise groups of scenes. In, for example, the fourth act of *The Private Tutor*, a number of very short scenes, set in two different places, are strung together, and the balanced antithesis which they establish is the message they contain. Nowhere in them does Lenz show himself directly, but he is clearly present in their juxtaposition. Like Lessing's, both plays use direct, colloquial prose, though interspersed with metaphoric passages of a kind rare in Lessing: and the social situations they describe are tragic without being in any sense aristocratic.

Lenz, like Lessing, matched his practice with theory, the most significant statement of which is his *Remarks about Theatre* (1771) in which Shakespeare serves as his model for an attack on Aristotle's *Poetics*. In the form of a lecture he takes up the central question of the relationship between plot and character: while Aristotle's observations suited the tragedy of his day, they are not appropriate for a different language and a different cultural period, an argument which rests squarely on Herder's claim that culture can only be understood as the product of a particular language at a particular time. Lenz, it must be admitted, is less than fair to Aristotle, but this does not matter greatly since his real purpose is expressed in his desire for 'freedom', a term of both political and aesthetic meaning.

> We are . . . or at least we want to be, the first rung on the ladder of free-acting, self-determining creatures and since we see a world before us and around us that is the proof of a boundless, free-acting being, so the very first impulse that we feel in our souls is the desire to imitate its example.[6]

Freedom is not just given the poet to create what he likes, but given by the poet to his characters to act of their own free will, and not be driven by the great 'puppet-show', as Büchner was to call it, fate. In writing, and later in defending *Danton* Büchner drew heavily on Lenz's arguments, especially in his understanding of Danton and the other 'bandits' of the revolution, as he calls them, as characters with their own free will over whom he, as author, has no control. He also modelled aspects of *Leonce* on the educational debate in *The Private Tutor* and the relationships between a town and its occupying garrison which forms the core of *The Soldiers* is a source for *Woyzeck*.

Schiller: the Pursuit of Freedom

Where Lenz had failed to impress Goethe with his plays, a factor in his ensuing breakdown, Friedrich Schiller (1759–1805)[7] who likewise suffered initially at the great man's disapproval, rose by his death to become the leading playwright of the German theatre and Goethe's closest friend.

Büchner's mother idolised Schiller and from an early age exposed her son to his work. Ironically it was later to be the immense popularity of Schiller's plays that were to constitute the greatest barrier to a recognition of Büchner's own talent.

Schiller preached freedom like Lessing and Lenz, but, under the influence of the philosophy of Immanuel Kant, stressed more the freedom of the spirit than that of the body. On this issue Büchner disagreed angrily with him, stressing the need for practical freedom. Schiller sprang overnight to fame at the age of twenty-three with his play *The Robbers* premiered at Mannheim in 1782. It was a success Büchner tried to emulate with *Danton*. An eye-witness described the theatre during the first night:

> The theatre was like a mad-house, rolling eyes, clenched fists, hoarse cries in the auditorium. Strangers fell weeping on each other's arms; women, near to fainting, stumbled to the doors. It was a general collapse like that in chaos whose fog brings forth new creative energy.[8]

By his own avowal, the work began a life-long debate with the writings of Shakespeare, but in his search for the secret of drama Schiller was drawn more to rules like Gottsched's than the freedom of Lenz, since, he argued, true freedom comes only through transcending not abandoning classical form.

For all Büchner's disagreement with Schiller they shared a preoccupation with the self, the purpose of life and the way the individual defines himself. This quest may be summarised as a quest for the meaning of *ich*, that word so highly charged in Büchner's *Lenz*. Franz, the evil brother of robber Moor, says, for example:

But I would like to ask *why* he made me? Surely not out of love for me, who must first become an *I*.[9]

In the understanding of that 'I' lies the understanding of the world, and Danton, Leonce and Woyzeck are similarly committed to its discovery. In *The Robbers* this discovery is mortal, killing both Franz, whom it drives mad, and his brother: it is likewise mortal to Louise and Ferdinand in *Kabale und Liebe* (1783) who only discover the truth about each other when irreversibly poisoned. In the much later *Wilhelm Tell* (1804) however, Tell finds himself in his duty to his country and the discovery is liberating.

Schiller also developed in his 'letters' *On the Aesthetic Education of Man* (1793) a theory of education that made an important contribution to Büchner's decision to use theatre as an educative weapon. Schiller saw in beauty the most effective method of education since it transcended the senses and the intellect: this enjoined the writer to subsume the logical and moral development of his 'argument' in 'play' and let immediate physical representation speak for him. The guillotine scene in *Danton* is an example of how this theory may be converted into practice – the 'aesthetic' effect far outweighing the tendentions.

Tieck: a New Theory of Comedy

The central figure in Büchner's immediate intellectual and theatrical environment was Ludwig Tieck (1773–1853) the most prolific, urbane and influential writer in Germany after Goethe's death in 1832, and well before that a challenger for his literary crown. The chief influences on him were Shakespeare and the rising interest in folk-song and legend, and in his play *Puss in Boots* (1797) he combines the two in a deft and witty manner. Büchner knew Tieck's work well, and through him came to read Lenz's plays which Tieck had been responsible for publishing.

Puss, drafted in a single night, is the first absurdist play in the German language. In it the boundary between audience and actor is broken, as much of the action takes place in the auditorium, where the 'spectators' have scripted comments on the 'play' that is being performed on stage. Set between 'audience' and 'actors' are the poet, in despair at the disastrous course the evening is taking, and the stage crew trying to follow his directions. To these are added musicians who take the play off, on occasion, into operatic parody. The result is that all the techniques of theatrical illusion are on display and the play works almost like a practical manual for the writer: this gives Tieck occasion to parody the more ridiculous aesthetic theories of the day, and Schiller takes his share of the jokes. At one point Fischer, a member of the 'audience', describes the actual story of Puss as 'a play-within-a-play', to indicate Tieck was consciously taking the logic of this Shakespearian device several steps further into what we know now as Absurdism.

Although the play promises well for the stage it was not performed until 1844 in Berlin, and then flopped. It was Jürgen Fehling, who directed *Woyzeck* in 1947, who was first to stage *Puss* successfully, in 1921: and it is perhaps no accident that Pirandello's *Six Characters in Search of an Author*, which is ponderous by comparison, first appeared in that year. Leavened by Tieck's wit, which certainly helped Büchner in writing *Leonce, Puss* is refreshingly light after the heavy dough of German classicism: it totally explodes any logic of plot, or indeed character, and directs the audience to consider a drama as what Lenz calls 'the interplay of the senses'.[10] It challenges us to see plot as that which happens in the theatre in a given space of time and to regard character as an arbitrary series of masks and disguises which are utterly transparent and utterly convincing. *Leonce* addresses itself to both this sense of plot and character, inconsistency and mask being of its essence.

Behind the practice lay a theory of comedy which Büchner himself used: this had four elements – strange or defamiliarised setting, variety of plot and character, a sense of limitless possibility for action engendered by constant interference and disruption, and a lot of music. All four Tieck claimed to find in Shakespeare. The practical dangers of the theory are clear in *Puss*: there is a huge variety of incident, the theatre as a place is defamiliarised, the plot is constantly disrupted and there is music; but there comes a point when too much variety can be simply tiresome. Büchner was aware of this trap and carefully avoided it in *Leonce*; more radically, he took the challenge to form which Tieck's work raised from the comic into the tragic sphere, so that when he considers terms like 'nature' and 'freedom' he does not mean some property of a distant enchanted isle, but Hessen in the 1830s. He also takes the techniques of disruption and alienation which in *Puss* are exclusively parodic and integrates them into the plots of all his plays, and in so doing deploys the 'alienation' effect (whose discovery is so often erroneously attributed to Brecht) as a dramatic device. Without Tieck's example this would not have been possible, but one of Büchner's chief gifts was to learn from the trials of others.

Grabbe: the Alienated Writer

Nowhere is this last skill more obvious, or more important than in Büchner's borrowings from Christian Dietrich Grabbe (1801–1836) a man whose life was almost as short, and no less tragic than Büchner's own. Büchner learned avidly from Grabbe; how to construct a play, how to focus a scene, how to suggest with limited forces unlimited power. Indeed, Grabbe's gift to Büchner was much like Gottsched's to Lessing, though given with more grace.

In a passage, now celebrated, from his Diaries of 1839, Hebbel compares Grabbe unfavourably with Büchner for lacking Büchner's intellectual stamina to draw a theme to its conclusion. The judgement is a harsh one: to praise Büchner need not be to attack Grabbe. Grabbe's plays are far longer than Büchner's and very rich, as I shall examine in two examples. Grabbe wrote his answer to Tieck's *Puss in 1822, Wit, Satire, Irony and Deeper Meaning*; in 1831 he wrote a sort of Hegelian version of a Schiller play *Napoleon or the Hundred Days*. Büchner borrowed from both.

In his titles alone the directions of Grabbe's thought are clear: in *Wit* he takes the exploded structure of *Puss* and starts to reconstruct it into a comedy that has a genuinely absurd plot, attacking in passing the mannerisms of such romantics as the Schlegels. In *Napoleon*, whose cast list seems to be the whole population of Europe in 1815, he takes theatre through towards the mammoth spectacles of Erwin Piscator's Berlin or D. W. Griffiths' Hollywood epics. Yet it also pursues Lessing's investigation of the formal relationship between the novel and drama, especially in its last half which reads like a Scott novel in dialogue and is extremely exciting.

The epic qualities of *Napoleon* are not confined to its historical scope for in it the trend of Lenz's work towards loosely episodic narrative moving forward by antithesis and implication is continued. By setting himself the task of putting such a huge topic as Napoleon on stage Grabbe had a similar problem to Büchner with the French Revolution, that of what to omit, and how to imply the full history from the chosen incidents. How too, does one 'stage' history without either belittling or ridiculing it simply by the grotesque reduction in scale? Grabbe's response is to start in a very tight analysis of the mood of the crowd in a corner of Paris and work outwards to Waterloo. His scenes are often long as a result and character takes a firm second place to the battles. The benefit to Büchner was that Grabbe had, in facing the difficulties of the source material, made it much easier for Büchner to make his own editorial decisions as well as giving him precise dramatic ideas to work with. Typical of these is the portrayal of the Paris mob hanging an innocent tailor from a lamp-post[11] which Büchner imitates, lamp-post and all, in the second scene of act one of *Danton*. Both scenes draw on a common source, the classic Shakespearian 'mob' scene, where the innocent poet Cinna is torn to pieces in *Julius Caesar*.

Even more revealing is the use of Grabbbe in a letter he wrote from Strasbourg to his family, the first that has survived. Büchner narrates the entry into the city of the Polish nationalist general Ramorino in terms that correspond closely to Grabbe's description of the entry of Napoleon into Paris:

As the rumour spread that Ramorino would travel through Strasbourg the students opened a subscription and decided to go out to meet him behind a black banner. [. . .] At last Ramorino appeared, accompanied by a whole crowd of riders; a student makes a speech, that he answers, as does a member of the national guard. The national guard form up round the carriage and draw it along; we place ourselves with the flag at the head of the column, in front of which marches a large band of musicians. And so we process into the city [. . .] singing the Marseillaise and the Carmagnole. Everywhere the cry reechoes Vive la liberté! [. . .] The city itself lights up, at the windows the women wave their shawls and Ramorino is drawn in triumph to his hotel where our standard-bearer hands him the flag with the wish that this funeral banner may soon turn itself into the standard of liberty. Thereupon Ramorino appears at the balcony, says thank-you, we cry long live Ramorino! – and the Comedy is complete.[12]

Allowing for the fact that Napoleon enters Paris a victor, the description in *Napoleon* is almost identical, the city 'lights up', the women wave their shawls and every gesture is decidedly theatrical. The most significant similarity is in the closing remark about the comedy, with its sudden withdrawal from the enthusiasms of the present tense to narrative distance. Likewise Grabbe's Jouve, who has commanded the Parisians to rejoice for Napoleon, suddenly says to himself: 'It's all just a comedy'.[13] Grabbe's love-hate relationship with both Napoleon and history – is it tragic or comic? – is one that Büchner had experienced both in person and in his writing. What perhaps makes Büchner better at getting it down on paper was his realisation, learning from Grabbe's mistakes, that it was not the task of theatre to put the Hegelian World-Historical person on stage in his public functions, when he merely embodied what the crowd wanted him to be, but rather in his private moments. History itself will take care of the battles and the mass-meetings, art will look to the moments in between. There is a suggestion that Grabbe knew this:

JOUVE: At home he [Napoleon] is, according to the way he feels, tetchy, witty, talkative like anyone else. If he goes out he masks himself, if he is at all uncertain of himself, first with the comedian's Talma game of expressions, or with practised furrows.[14]

Here is both the mask which *Danton* explores and the metaphor of the political leader as actor. When Büchner writes *Danton*, in effect he overlays the public figure with the observing character of a Jouve so that Danton becomes both chief protagonist and chorus in his own tragedy.

In *Wit* the tension between participation in the action on its own terms and sudden withdrawal to a position of comment is exploited to grotesque and comic purpose both linguistically and structurally. The most obvious example is the sudden obscenity which upsets the smooth politeness of the discourse: but this is part of a much more ambitious plan to reveal the World Spirit in all aspects of the age. On this subject Grabbe is quite explicit: 'If the reader does not find a decisive world view at the base of this comedy it deserves no praise. And by the way, it jokes about itself, and the various literary sallies will be forgiven for that very reason.'[15] It does indeed take a much keener knife to its age than Tieck's *Puss*, but the final joke when Grabbe himself appears, underlines the fact that he, too, is to blame. The scene is striking: Grabbe comes at night to a lonely house in the middle of a wood and he bears a lantern, to the derision of all present. What an image of his alienation! And yet what a defiant claim to be the one source of light.[16]

The plot is close in spirit to Ben Jonson both in the variety and in the nature of its incident: there is a duped ass of a devil, a lot of puns and clichés, and a story that dissolves into a form of studied anarchy. The real purpose, however, is vituperative:

> MORDAX: The muse of tragedy has become a gutter-whore since every German trickster rapes her at will and gets of her five-legged moon calves.[17]

This sudden break into obscenity from the suave aristocratic manner of the Baron cuts right across the wit and geniality and reminds the reader of the deadly seriousness of the play: if tragedy has become debased, the whole of society's moral strength is debased with it. This debasement reflects itself in the 'jokes' the Devil tells, one of which is the fourteen-year 'shaggy-dog' story of the French Revolution. 'The play was particularly badly received, not least because it had the mistaken habit of guillotining its critics.'[18] The Devil goes further: 'And so I must tell you that this quintessence of the universe that you honour by the name of world is nothing but a second rate comedy.'[19] In this comedy one further incident stands out, a scene with no words, when the Freiherr Mordax goes for a walk: in accordance with his compact with the devil he murders thirteen tailors' apprentices, and then, pleased with his morning's activity, saunters home.[20] In its casually turned horror the image smacks of the language of the *Courier* and of Woyzeck's vision of a world laughing and drinking while the bloody head creeps across the grass.

Wit was first performed successfully in 1907 under Max Halbe, the same man who first staged *Leonce*. Both Büchner and Grabbe benefited from the shift of theatrical opinion in the last years of the nineteenth century. Nor is it coincidence that Grabbe's death from alcoholism should have similarities with Lenz's, both men testifying to the deep disorientation felt by sensitive men in Germany as the age of the Enlightenment drew to a close. The problem that they faced, especially when they wrote about history was that there were no values they could affirm: while Shakespeare had around him the lively image of an ascendant state towards which the history he wrote about was moving, Lenz, Grabbe and Büchner had nothing but decline to lament. Even Napoleon, Grabbe's hero, was brought low; even the great Danton, saviour of France was guillotined. Was it any wonder then to find understanding only in the debris of civilisation, the Woyzecks?

Nature poetry: Shakespeare, Goethe and German Cultural Identity

Intimately related to the dissenting pursuit of freedom in the theatre was a movement in Germany towards 'nature' and especially towards the folk-song. The chief philosopher of this movement was Johann Herder (1744–1803) who saw in folk-song and nature poetry the satisfaction of the need of a strong, unbroken, young and nature-bound soul to express its feelings in metaphors.[21] These metaphors were natural because accessible to all. The role of the great writer, notably Shakespeare, was to synthesise this natural instinct for metaphor with tragedy, thus uniting 'nature' with 'art', and in this Goethe followed his example.[22] But Goethe was by no means alone, since, under Herder's influence, many writers realised that the discovery of a native German cultural tradition shared by all the German-speaking states would be a necessary prerequisite to the political movement for unity.

Initially, interest in nature reflected itself in what we would now understand as highly literary falsifications of the original folk-material, such as those printed by Clemens Brentano and Achim von Arnim in *Des Knaben Wunderhorn* (1806), still among the best known of German poems. Poets like Goethe and Schiller, whose *Heidenröslein* and *Die Glocke* respectively are the German equivalent of Wordsworth's *Daffodils*, also consciously imitated the folk style. But it was Büchner's use of folk-song which made it into a politically loaded form of protest against oppression. Of course, Schiller's Swiss in *Tell* sing songs full of the witness of their own national pride, but all they sing is vested with the consciousness of freedom. Büchner's Hessians sing without even knowing that what expresses itself in their song is the desire for freedom: Büchner realised that when Andres sings of the hunter riding through the woods in spring that what he really wants is to stop being hunted himself.

The political implications of nature – the desire to be 'free' – are balanced in Shakespeare by the personal: the reflection of a man's nature in the world around him. The attention so many writers paid to *King Lear* stemmed from their realisation that in it Shakespeare had fused the private and political aspects of nature and thereby opened up a whole new world of imagery, an experience in which both Büchner and Goethe revelled. Goethe explores this new world in his educational novel *Wilhelm Meister* in which the apprentice playwright, Meister, learns from the real *Meister*, Shakespeare.[23] The importance of this work for its time cannot be overstated and for Büchner it laid out the boundaries of two central areas of concern: the role of theatre in the education of the general public and the function of writing for the stage in his own inner development.

After a brief flirtation with an actress, the young Wilhelm runs away from home to join an acting troupe and his education consists in writing and performing for this company. The key figure in his education becomes Hamlet, the most richly metaphoric of all Shakespeare's characters and one whom Wilhelm is asked to play. (Leonce also imitates Hamlet.) At first Wilhelm is concerned with Hamlet's appearance, whether or not he should be, as a Dane, blond and blue-eyed. Then he delves into his character and here Goethe offers a theory that has much in common with Büchner's theoretical perception of Woyzeck:

A beautiful, pure, noble, highly moral spirit, without the nervous strength that makes heroes is broken down by a burden that it can neither carry nor throw off; every duty is sacred to him, but this one too onerous. The impossible is asked of him; not something in itself impossible, but what for him is impossible.[24]

Woyzeck is clearly no intellectual, nor able to articulate the burden on him with Hamlet's fluency, but there is much in his struggle with nature to link it with Hamlet's, as seen by Goethe. In Büchner's terms, this link is expressive of shared intuitions of deep natural truths, those truths Lenz searches for in the Vosges and in the writings of Shakespeare.

In *Wilhelm Meister* there is a discussion of the relative virtues of the novel and the drama and the different types of language they use. In the conclusions reached are the seeds of Büchner's (and Grabbe's) trick of alienation – that sudden withdrawal from engagement in the action to comment on it. Drama is in essence about action, and the novel about comment:

Above all sentiments and events are to be presented in the novel: in drama, characters and actions. The novel must proceed slowly and the sentiments of the characters must, in whatever way they will, interrupt the urge of the whole to develop. The drama should move fast and the character of the main protagonist must press forward to the end and only be interrupted. The novelistic hero must suffer and not, at least in any high degree, act: of the dramatic hero one demands effects and deeds.[25]

The problem that *Hamlet* sets is that it is a play that appears to obey the rules of the novel, and it is a mark of Büchner's radicalism that he understood this and consciously imitated the dynamic principle of the novel as described by Goethe in his plays, while maintaining the speed Goethe requires of the play.

Immermann's Musterbühne (1832–38)

Goethe died in 1832 and in that year an admirer, Karl Immermann, a Prussian civil servant, started a series of public readings of plays, including Goethe's, in the city of Düsseldorf. Immermann hoped to steer German theatre back to the style developed by Goethe during his time as theatre director in Weimar, a style that during the Napoleonic Wars had completely died out. The rapid rise and fall of this enterprise is almost exactly contemporaneous with Büchner's writing career and the ideals for which Immermann worked, and the reasons why they failed, of direct relevance to it.[26]

Immermann's readings were so successful that by October 1832 he was able to found a theatre society, and by February 1833 the *Musterbühne* – 'classic theatre' – was in action, opening with a production of Lessing's *Emilia Galotti* (1772). Goethe, Schiller, Lessing, Shakespeare and Calderon formed the core of the diet. In late 1834 for example, *Macbeth* opened on 2 November and *Hamlet* on 28 December. But after the excitement of the first two years the theatre began to falter, not helped by the fact that Immermann had to run it in addition to his full load of administrative work. By 1838 the *Musterbühne* was dead.

In returning to the Goethean ideals of Weimar, Immermann pursued a directorial policy that concentrated first on the actors' words, ensuring perfect delivery and intonation before transferring to the stage. On stage itself movement was added, but of a precise, pantomimic sort designed to establish a provocative tension or counterpoint between word and action whose purpose was the realisation of the

Hegelian dialectic in performance, drama being the syn-
thetic resolution of the dialectic of words and actions,
speech and movement. Immermann insisted, as had
Goethe, on his actors knowing about the literary context
and value of what they were performing, so that the performance could be educational not simply entertaining.
Düsseldorf was a good place to try such an experiment,
open as it was to new influences through a long period of
Napoleonic occupation and, in 1830, caught by the fever of
the Glorious Days. But as the hopes of change that those
events brought faded in the following decade, so did the
optimism of Immermann's theatre.

There were other reasons. Mass tastes in the theatre seldom coincide with high intellectual demands and the
attempt to revive the performance mode of a past generation is beset with difficulties. What attracts audiences is the
novelty value, which, once gone, is no substitute for a con-
sidered artistic policy. Immermann could offer no such policy. All over Germany the works of August von Kotzebue
(1716–1819), Wilhelm Iffland (1759–1814) and, in Vienna,
Edward Bauernfeld (1802–1890) were by far the most
successful writers and their formulae, endlessly varied, of
trite morality and virtue rewarded was well suited to the
self-satisfied audiences they served.[27] Even high-minded
Immmermann bowed to this pressure when, amid the classics he had works performed by the then highly popular
Ernst Raupach, a writer who would now be forgotten but,
perhaps, for Heine's jokes at his expense. In other words,
the pedestrian and constrictive world of Darmstadt, cap-
tured by Luise Büchner, was typical of Germanic culture.

Complementary to moral comedy was the grandiose
national spectacle, about Germanic feats and suggestive of
artistic racial theories which were to surface in the works of
Richard Wagner and later in the Third Reich. Nor was this

interest in grandiosity confined to the stage: the building of
the Viennese Ring owes much to the spacious perspectives
of the contemporary scene painter; and in Germany the
best architect, Karl Friedrich Schinkel, was also the best set
designer, talents which he combined in his work on Burg
Rheinstein and the completing of Köln cathedral. More
popularly grandiosity also led to a new interest in parades,
ceremonial marches, carnival processions and political
demonstrations, nearly all of which were organised for the
benefit of the ruling dignitaries. All these tendencies,
though with a totally different emphasis are reflected in
Büchner's writing: in *Danton* the guillotine, and the ceremonial that attends it, celebrates the demise of absolutism;
in *Leonce* the peasants parade in front of their prince to
honour his wedding; and in *Woyzeck* the curfew march is
the beginning of Marie's fatal liaison with the Drum-major.
And, as we have seen, a decisive moment in Büchner's own
political education was Ramorino's entry into Strasbourg.
Likewise, the sets demanded by his plays are huge – major
public buildings, reception rooms on the one hand, and distant perspectives of the city on the other.

While Immermann failed to satisfy his public on either
the moral or the grandiose count, he did provide them with
a centre of public attention, one ray of light in a gloomy
picture. It was sometimes remarked that the theatre had
taken over from parliament the charge of public debate, a
remark which drew attention as much to the lack of a parliament as to the political function of theatre. In like manner,
the Austrian writer Grillparzer observed: 'Now that people
no longer go to church, the theatre is the only public place
of worship left.'[28] As the century progressed German
politics became increasingly influenced by the resurgent
myth of Germanic national strength and destiny, a resur-
gence to which the theatre contributed. Büchner realised

this was happening but hoped that by presenting history objectively and forcefully on stage he could redirect resurgent nationalism towards a new spirit of brotherhood and equity. The attempt was misconceived. After the *Courier* affair Büchner must have known the difficulties he faced, but he was not entirely prepared for the disapproval that greeted his *Danton*.

4
Danton's Death

Danton's Death must be the most remarkable first play in European culture. Until January 1835 there is no evidence that Büchner had ever tried his hand at the theatre, no history of family theatrical entertainments, no puppet shows like those staged by the boy Goethe. Yet in the space of five weeks Büchner wrote a play that, especially since the great production by Max Reinhardt in 1916, has become a classic of the German theatre and is seldom out of the repertoire of at least one major company. In its day the work won him little recognition: some thought he had merely edited his main source, Auguste Thiers' *Histoire de la Révolution Francaise* (1823–27), into actable form; others, especially the Darmstadt middle class, were shocked and disgusted by the play's obscenity and common language. The play certainly is blunt, but only, as Büchner argued, because its historical counterparts were blunt.

The historical source for the central figure is Georges Jacques Danton (1759–94), a lawyer who shot to prominence during the first Revolutionary phase in Paris in

1789.[1] Through a mixture of cunning, will-power, and stirring oratory he quickly established a power base in the lower classes of Paris and was largely responsible for the move to arrest the royal family in August 1792. In September 1792 he was Justice Minister and one of the most powerful figures in the state, but he failed to use his influence to prevent the so-called 'September murders', a purge of senior army personnel. This memory was to haunt him. In March 1793 he was largely instrumental in setting up the three main organs of Revolutionary government, the Tribunal, the Court and the Public Welfare Committee. Although himself a Jacobin, he hoped to achieve some sort of compromise with the more moderate Girondiste party, and at the same time forge alliances abroad, both of which policies brought him into conflict with Robespierre and into increasing political isolation. Early in 1794 Robespierre felt powerful enough to move against him and had him guillotined on 4 April 1794.

Danton's single greatest achievement was more the result of his oratory and will-power than his cunning. As a result of the 'September murders' and the chaos in the Parisian administration the Revolutionary militia armies were effectively leaderless and demoralised. He alone was able to persuade them of their ability to fight and win, and this they did at the tactically insignificant skirmish of Valmy on 20 September 1792. Here the Revolutionary army was able to check the advance of the Prussian and Royalist forces, a strategic and psychological catastrophe to the proud Prussians. Goethe, who watched with amazement, wrote: 'From here and today has begun a new chapter in the history of the world.'[2] He was right, and Danton was the man who turned the page.

Büchner mentions most of these high-points of Danton's life but all in retrospect: his work begins at the start of Danton's overthrow by Robespierre. What interests him is the private side of Danton, the temperament that was able to rescue France but not himself. He analyses how a revolutionary leader functions and how he can be seduced into becoming in himself almost a symbol of what he set out to overthrow. He shows us little action, little heroism, little fervour and much that is only hinted at in the historical sources available to him: yet it is in his awareness of how to deploy those sources that he most obviously reveals his talent. In his hands, source material becomes something entirely new, even when he quotes word for word, because he recognised the essential power of dramatic context to define and redefine meaning. To elucidate this process I shall examine the play's scenic structure in the context of the tradition of dissent I described in my previous chapter, in which Büchner carries the fight against neo-classicism further than any of his predecessors.

Plot

Even in terms of Aristotle's simplest statement about plot as 'nothing more or less than the combination of the incidents or things done in the story' the distance between tragedy as he analyses it in the *Poetics* and Büchner's understanding of the term is obvious. Danton is mostly 'done to' and his heroism consists largely in his passivity. He is first shown as a debauched gambler, a revolutionary athlete gone to fat, whose enemies are closing in. He tries to compromise with Robespierre, their leader, but Robespierre senses his weakness and refuses. He contemplates escape and suicide, while his friends urge him to action; but when he does act it is too late. Finally he resigns himself to accepting what history has done with him and that his path is to the guillotine and death. With each of Aristotle's more complex propositions the gap between this 'action' and any classical ideal grows, for which Büchner has been criticised. *Danton* is seen as an 'anti-play', a tragedy with no hero: but just these features have led to a contrary belief that it is the first modern play, a documentary account in which 'plot' is shown as not necessarily synonymous with action and that thought is as much action as standing up and fighting.

Aristotle requires a play to have a 'beginning, a middle and an end': *Danton* begins at the end of the 'middle' and seems like one long 'end'. Its main character is largely passive. The plot is designed to reveal this passivity in all its strength, and here most decisively Büchner adopts an anti-Aristotelian stance. For Aristotle, 'tragedy is an imitation not of persons but of action and life, of happiness and misery. Now happiness and misery take the form of action; the end at which the dramatist aims is a certain kind of activity, not a quality.' What Büchner achieves, however, is a 'quality': how is this done?

Büchner's trademark is most visible in the scenic arrangement based on a strategy of contrast. There are four acts, each having a varied number of scenes: the action does not obey the unity of place in a literal sense at all, and time is handled in a Shakespearian manner where the whole action could be the work of a few hours or of some weeks. There are very few precise references to time in the present, but many to time past. This conflict between an ever present past and a strangely vacant present is complemented by a conflict between the public showplace and the private room and between life indoors and outdoors. At one crucial point the action moves outside the city into the country.

These conflicts of time and place offer the emblematic context for a clash of wills, at first Danton's with Robespierre's but increasingly Danton's past with his present.

This has a thoroughly Shakespearian feel: but in one technical detail Büchner reveals his inexperience in staging that all his Shakespearian grounding did not help him avoid. On a number of occasions Danton leaves the stage at the end of a scene only to have to return to it immediately for the next, which is set in a different part of Paris. In television or film this is easy to manage: one cross cuts or fades. But while the device keeps our attention *de facto* on Danton it does mean that the smooth, naturalistic surface of the narrative is constantly interrupted. This can lead on stage to long gaps for scene changes when speed is the order of the day. The interruptive strategy is conscious, reminding us time and again of the fact that the true text of the play is metaphoric. But it raises the question whether *Danton* should be staged in its existing form, or whether it is not rather a drama for the mind. To answer this I shall first look at certain aspects of its scenic structure, which I have presented in tabular form (Table 4.1).

TABLE 4.1

Act/scene	Place	Characters/ Groups	Time	Indoors/ Outdoors
1.1	Casino/Café	Danton + allies, Whores	early evening?	In/private
1.2	Street	Commoners, Robespierre	unclear	Out/public
1.3	Jacobin Club	Robespierre + allies	unclear	In/public
1.4	Street	Leaders	unclear	Out/private
1.5	A room	Danton, Marion	day/night	In/private
1.6	A room	Danton, Robespierre	night	In/private
2.1	A room	Danton, allies	early morning?	In/private

2.2	A Promenade	Danton, Citizens	unclear	Out/public
2.3	A room	Danton, Lucile, Camille	unclear	In/private
2.4	A FIELD	Danton	unclear	Out/private
2.5	A room	Danton, Julie	NIGHT (only clear reference to time in stage directions)	In/private
2.6	A street	Citizens–Soldiers	night	Out/public
2.7	National Convent	Deputies, Leaders	unclear	In/public
3.1	Luxembourg prison	Fallen leaders	middle of night?	In/public
3.2	A room	Leaders	unclear	In/private
3.3	A corridor, Conciergerie	Danton, Prisoners	unclear	In/public
3.4	Tribunal	Danton, Court	unclear	In/public
3.5	Luxembourg	Dillon, Laflotte	unclear	In/private
3.6	Committee of Public Welfare	St Just + allies	unclear	In/public
3.7	Conciergerie	Danton + allies	unclear	In/public
3.8	A room	Danton's enemies	unclear	In/private
3.9	Tribunal	Danton on trial	unclear	In/public
3.10	Square in front of Palais de Justice	People	unclear	Out/public
4.1	A room	Julie	unclear	In/private
4.2	A street	Citizens	unclear	Out/public
4.3	Conciergerie	Danton + allies	night	Inside
4.4	Square in front of Conciergerie	People, Lucile	early morning?	Out/public
4.5	Conciergerie	Danton + allies	early morning	In/public
4.6	A room	Julie	early morning	In/private

4.7	Place de la Revolution	People, Danton + allies	early morning	Out/public
4.8	A street	Lucile	unclear	Out/private
4.9	Place de la Revolution	Executioners, Lucile	unclear	Out/public

The organisation of the scenes is plainest in the last column in which the tension between inside and outside and private and public is clear: the real decisions of the Republic are taken inside, in private, and the effects felt outside, in public. The people in whose name decisions are made are always outside waiting and the only connecting points between leaders and led are in the street or the casino, by accident, or through the agency of whores. As Büchner said, the most cosmopolitan things in the world are whores and liberty, and to these one might add a third, death, a figure whom Danton sees as the most promiscuous of all whores, for she sleeps with us all.

Bearing the last column in mind the most striking feature of the 'place' list is that there is only one non-urban environment. Büchner obviously meant this scene (2, 4) to be especially important: the one moment when Danton is weakening towards action, that is running away, he goes out into the open fields, into nature. Here he feels at arm's length from death. Yet he does not escape, and his return is to certain death. The city, viewed at a distance, takes on the role of the maker of human history and values while the field stands for those forces which challenge history in its man-made sense.

The city itself has two aspects, the public and the private, and each of these has its respective locations: the tribunal, club or committee is a public place while the bedroom is private, especially in its sexual function. Occasionally a public place may be made private by virtue of a special circumstance, like intrigue, and private places may be invaded by public, like Danton's bedroom. These infringements are however, deliberate indications of movements in the political world, which has the power to reach all but the most intimate moments of sexual freedom. Danton, who is forced out of his private world into the public places of confrontation comes to realise that all political power is a myth since no one actually has the ability to influence the natural course of events. Büchner's clearest implicit statement to this effect is that none of the leaders who deposed Danton witnesses his death, implying that Danton is not their victim but that his death lies in the nature of the Revolution.

The people, seen in the street waiting or whoring, rest uneasily between the private domains of their leaders. From their perspective the Tribunal is every bit as private as Danton's house. At critical moments in the play they intrude into the political battle and remind their leaders, and the audience, that they still do not have enough to eat for all the guillotined heads, a motif taken straight from the *Courier*. This reversal of perspective is a classic Büchnerian device.

There are other moments in the plot which lie on the boundary between in and out and public and private, where city and nature and day and night meet. These thresholds or 'liminal' moments contain the play's most richly metaphoric meanings. Three dominate: twice Danton stands at a window, as does Robespierre once, and looks out into the night. Danton's first window speech comes directly after his visit to the field (2, 5): as he looks out into the night towards the place from which he has come night and day, past and present, dream and reality, the country and the city and 'in' and 'out' meet and he is gripped by a feverish breakdown. This boundary state is brief, but in it his mind is laid open with clinical precision. On the second occasion (4, 5) he is in prison but calm by contrast and resigned to accept the lessons of his previous experience at a window. This calm is tested when his friend Camille, with him in prison, experiences at the window just the same terror as Danton earlier on. Camille is hoping to see Lucile for the last time, but dreams that the night sky has come down to touch the earth and the moon has turned into a huge harbinger of death, both of which visions remind him of his impending execution. Danton soothes him and passes his personal test.

The key to both Danton's and Camille's terror lies in Robespierre's one private speech, also spoken at night at a window (1,6), which is the first of all the play's liminal moments.

> ROBESPIERRE: And isn't our waking a dream only with more light; aren't we sleep-walkers; isn't our action like that of a dream only clearer, more certain, executed more purposefully? [. . .] In one hour the spirit imagines more deeds of thought than the sluggish organism of our body can accomplish in years.

The language is full of that same impatient energy that characterises Lenz's first appearance, the wish to achieve things at immense speed: and in Robespierre's vision Büchner makes clear how night and day, dream and waking, thought and action are but phases of a continuous natural process that one can neither speed up nor slow down. Even life and death are in this relationship with one another, suggesting that truly to live is to be always half in the grave.

The street and the promenade are used in a more covert way than the window as boundary states, mid-way between the open field and the closed room and suggestive of day-time in contrast to the night time at the window. In the promenade a young man talks of love and nature, the only such time in the play when these two forces seem to have a positive aspect. In the back-street the people meet their leaders, a boundary place that ironises the true nature of politics.

Such ironies are the most accessible evidence in the play of its 'shadow' structure which locates all experience in both life and art in the context of death and the annihilation of the individual. Danton knows from the outset that the Revolution is an illusion, that time itself is a man-made illusion which resolves itself into an endless sequence of dressing and undressing. Even love reminds him of death:

> DANTON: (to Julie) People say that in the grave is rest and that the grave and rest are the same thing: if that is true I lie already buried in your lap. You sweet grave, your lips are the bells of death, your voice a funeral peal, your breast my burial mound and your heart my cask.
>
> LADY: Lost!   (1, 1)

Though the lady's remark is part of another conversation, it comments directly on what Danton has just said, for Danton is indeed lost. Only in death does life achieve meaning, but death has the power to transform all meanings into itself. *Danton* strikes out in the opposite direction to *Oedipus*: in Revolutionary Paris there is no personal guilt as in Thebes, no moral expiation, only natural suffering and human pity. And even these last qualities are exposed as selfish, standing in the way of man's understanding the true natural purpose of his existence. The whole strategy of the plot tends to undermine the play's title, for it is ultimately irrelevant to the plot whether Danton lives or dies.

Character

Second to plot in Aristotle's analysis of the constituents of tragedy is character, second because character is tested and revealed through action. This statement is then qualified by a description of the sort of figure suitable for tragedy:

> The plot, in the finest form of tragedy, must not be simple but complex; and further, it must imitate actions that arouse pity and fear. Consequently i) a good man must not be shown as passing from happiness to misfortune; for that does not inspire pity or fear, but is an outrage upon our moral feeling. Nor ii) must a bad man be seen passing from misfortune to happiness. That is as untragic as can possibly be; it makes no appeal to our sense of poetic justice, or to our pity or to our fear. Nor iii) should an extremely bad man be depicted as falling from happiness to misfortune.[3]

His analysis rests on the primacy of a moral code, external to the plot, against which conduct can be measured. Büchner is at his most radical in rejecting such a code, or indeed any system of analysis, that contains ideological conceptions prejudicial to his one guiding principle that actions have no other meanings than themselves. This is not to say his work does not arouse pity and fear, those two emotions that Aristotle sees at the heart of the cathartic purpose of tragedy; but Büchner uses them as a means to another end, namely their eventual rejection as irrelevant. He first hints he will do this when Danton goes to the field, where not pity and fear but time and nature count most:

> DANTON: This place is supposed to be safe, perhaps for my memory, but not for me. The grave gives me more

safety, it brings me the chance at least to forget. It kills my memory. But there my memory lives and it kills me. Me or it? The answer is easy. (*He gets up and turns back*) I'm flirting with death: it's quite pleasant to make eyes at her from a distance, through a lorgnette. I ought really to laugh at the whole thing. There's a sense of continuance in me that says tomorrow will be like today and the day after that and beyond that everything is like it is now. (2, 4)

When Danton gets up to return it is with a mixture of Macbeth's final heroism and Seneca's stoicism, not untinged by an epicurean interest in death as an experience, or rather *the* experience of life. He knows that neither his nor any other individual life matters to history, but at least by way of compensation one may at any time, through suicide, remove himself from the historical process. In returning to Paris, Danton accepts a long 'suicide' and is able to watch his own decision taking effect. What is striking however, is, to use Macbeth's acting metaphor, that his understanding of himself suddenly sharpens when he steps outside his role as revolutionary leader rather than being found through that role. This in turn suggests that the way to approach playing the part is not through naturalistic character building, or still worse, identification, but cool observation of his behaviour and a distanced reproduction of it.

The most distinctive feature of the second column in my table of scenes is what is missing – the sense of heroic conflict. Danton and Robespierre could, like Antony and Octavian, be shown fighting for the world: but Robespierre appears only in the first act, and then more as catalyst than reagent. It is remarkable how much attention producers and critics focus on Robespierre, but only in his window scene does he have any speech of real significance. At the

Jacobin club he speaks in formulae and those formulae are the words of the present state of the Revolution. If he did not utter them someone else would. At the window he acknowledges, only to reject, that there is a sphere where these formulae do not reach, sexual relations, but he turns his sexual energy loose in the Terror, for him a long orgasm of bloodshed.

The sexual sphere is dominated by those outside the political circle, the women Julie, Marion and Lucile. All three are richly sensual and giving, and all three embody that view of sexuality that Ludwig Feuerbach was soon to formulate as the first and only true motive force in the world: this force unites lovers, families, communities and nations both because it drives individuals into association with other individuals and because it is a property with which all are endowed irrespective of rank. The decisive statement on the centrality of sexuality is given to Marion in a speech of comparable compactness and significance to Ulysses' disquisition on 'degree' in *Troilus and Cressida*. I quote almost the whole passage because in it are distilled nearly all the classic features of Büchner's mind:

My mother was a clever woman; she always told me that chastity was a beautiful virtue. When people came to the house and started talking about certain things she ordered me out of the room. If I asked what they meant she told me I should be ashamed of myself. If she gave me a book to read there were nearly always passages for me to skip. But I could read what I liked in the Bible, it was Holy Writ. There was a thing in it I could not understand. I didn't like asking anybody so I brooded it out by myself. Then the spring came; something was happening all around me in which I had no part. I slipped into a strange atmosphere which stifled me almost. I looked at my own limbs. Sometimes I felt as if I were two separate people, then the two melted into one again. About that time a young fellow used to come to our house. [. . .] My mother asked him more often, and that suited us very well. Finally we couldn't see why we shouldn't lie next to each other between two sheets just as well as sit with each other on two chairs. I found more pleasure in this than in his talk and I could not see why we should be allowed the smaller pleasure and denied the greater. We did it secretly. And so it went on. But I became like the sea that devours everything and drags it deeper and deeper. There was only one contrast for me and all men melted into one body. It was my nature. How can you escape yourself? In the end he noticed. One morning he came and kissed me; as if he were going to strangle me he wound his arms around my neck. [. . .] Then he left; again I did not know what he wanted. That evening I sat by the window; I am very sensitive. I am connected with things around me only by my feelings. I submerged in the waves of the sunset. A crowd came down the street with children running in front and women staring out of the windows. I looked down; they carried him by in a basket; the moon shone on his white forehead, his hair was wet, he had drowned himself. I had to cry. This was the only flaw in my being. Other people have Sundays and weekdays, they work six days and pray on the seventh. They are moved once a year on their birthdays and think about themselves once a year on New Year's Eve; I can't grasp all that. I know nothing about divisions or changes. There is only one thing for me: a continual longing and grasping, a glow, a stream. My mother died of grief; people point their fingers at me. That is stupid. There is only one thing which counts, what you feel most pleasure in; in bodies, pictures of

Christ, flowers or toys. The feeling is just the same. The
greater your pleasure the more you pray.   (1, 5)

Marion's implicit defence of her nature is of a piece with
Danton's and indeed there is much to suggest she is a product of Danton's mind since they both share the same belief
in 'nature'. But Marion's relationship with nature is far
more developed than Danton's – she reacts with the spring
and compares herself to the sea. She is also deeply preoccu-
pied with her body, not from lecherous or disgusted
motives but because she knows that her body defines her
self and hence her nature. Büchner the 'pathologist' is
pleading through her for a more scientific approach to
bodily sensation not a sacriligious or obscene one, but he
must have been naive to think that good Darmstadt citizens
would not be offended at the direct coalition of prayer and
pleasure.

Now it is more Marion's apparent callousness than her
sacrilege which jolts: how can she call her grief at her
lover's death a flaw? She sees the reflection of the moon on
his wet forehead, that same moon of death in Camille's
dream, but this very reflection tells her that his suicide is as
much 'natural' as her distance from him. It is a flaw to
grieve because grief attempts to erect a moral edifice on the
natural act of suicide. In its radicalism this view looks forward both to Büchner's own work *Woyzeck* and to Ludwig
Feuerbach's influential treatise *The Essence of Christianity*
(1842), begun some four years after *Danton* was written.

Feuerbach was a pupil of Hegel's who, like Büchner,
began to question some of the basic premises of Hegelian
thought, especially those dealing with the state's right over
the individual and the place of the absolute 'World Spirit' in
the ordering of human conduct. Not the state's but the individual's rights and needs are Feuerbach's concern. Hegel's

God is no more than a wish-fulfilling projection of all those things men cannot do by themselves and a compensation for man's disappointment at the weakness of his fellows. For Feuerbach it is not the World Spirit which runs men's lives but the sexual drive. The individual finds his fulfilment first in the sexual act, in sensations and sensory perceptions. 'The characteristic feature of the modern age,' argues Feuerbach 'is that in it the human being as human being, the person as person, and thereby the separate human individual has been recognised as god-like and eternal in himself and in his individuality.'[4] In these terms it is no longer blasphemy to compare prayer with making love because each individual in expressing himself in this way effectively 'prays' to himself. Nor is the individual guilty of a sin of pride in this since the overwhelming power of the sexual drive forces him to participate with another person in the most important of all his acts – loving. 'In the satisfaction of my other instincts I am completely in control; I need the object of my desire solely for my own benefit; I have admittedly got needs, but in the satisfaction of my need I intend the destruction of that object. But in the sexual drive I fulfil myself as a part, that because it is only a part seeks its completion. To start with I certainly am looking for pleasure, but I cannot gain that pleasure without making myself a substratum, a means of pleasure for the object of my desire.'[5] Feuerbach sees all human activity, especially social, as coming from this conscious part-disavowal of one's individual self and its transfusion into the life of a sexual union, of a family, of a community. From this derives, by a process of sublimation, the urge to think, to speak and to converse. Philosophy is seen as a form of abstract copulation of minds, a complete submergence of the individual in the dialogue.[6] By no means is sexuality the be all and end all of Feuerbach's philosophy, nor indeed of Büchner's.

One particular junction between philosophy and sexuality is vitally important to Büchner, the love-suicide: this is not for him the grandiose singing of Wagner's *Tristan and Isolde* but the quiet resignation, very much in private, of Julie and Lucile, both of whom choose death rather than outlive their lovers. When this sincere love was misunderstood by his Darmstadt critics he was most upset, and in his reply he tackles both the question of obscenity and, in Aristotelian terms, the problem of character and morality in general:

> With regard to the so-called immorality of my play I would answer as follows. In my eyes the dramatic poet is nothing but an historiographer, but he is *superior* to the latter because he [. . .] instead of giving us a dry account, puts us into the life of the past as if it were happening now. Instead of giving us characteristics he gives us characters and instead of descriptions he gives us human beings [. . .] His book must not be *more* or *less moral* than *history itself* [. . .] I can't turn Danton and the bandits of the Revolution into heroes of virtue! [. . .] If some obscene expressions occur, consider the notoriously obscene language of the time, of which my play gives only a weak impression [. . .] As for the so-called idealist poets, they create nothing but marionettes with sky-blue noses and affected pathos, not men of flesh and blood, whose suffering and joy we can share and whose actions fill us with horror or admiration. In a word I think much of Goethe and Shakespeare but little of Schiller.'[7]

The use of Aristotle is carefully differentiated, as the following passage from *The Poetics* shows: 'Where the historian really differs from the poet is in his describing what has happened, while the other describes the sort of thing that might happen. Poetry therefore is more philosophic and of greater significance than history, for its statements are of the nature rather of universals, whereas those of history are particulars.' Büchner agrees with Aristotle in ranking the poet above the historian but because of his ability to represent the natural order of things not for the superiority of his moral insights. Yet, as *Danton* shows, the poet can actually undertake both tasks, using historically accurate material but still showing how Danton might well have felt in private. Büchner was liberating poetry from the historical detail in which it was bound through the agency of natural law and not, like Aristotle's poet, through moral stricture.

His argument is however, inconsistent with the stress he places on the 'puppet-show' of history, not least when he criticises the idealists for their puppets. When he praises characters above characteristics he seems to be pleading for a freedom of will which directly contradicts the natural law which he so vigorously proposes. The difficulty is located in Revolutionary history itself: we all know that Danton went to the guillotine, and any play about this subject is prey to two dangers. Either it may belittle the historical events by over-simplification or excessive attention to artistic rather than historical truth, or it may work like a preprogrammed action that is untragic because it denies choice. Of necessity therefore, the play has to negotiate between the inevitability of the end – the guillotine – and the many ways of presenting how that end is reached. With the exception of Danton, it is notable that all the male characters in the play seem to be part of an historical process in a way the women are not and significantly the women exercise what seem for Büchner to be the two great freedoms of natural law, suicide and making love. Danton is shown as moving from what is the 'male' principle of inevitable submission to historical destiny towards a 'female' principle of freedom through submission to nature. Büchner takes us through this process with him and allows us to see with Danton's eyes not our own. We are thus submerged in meanings other than those offered by the surface of historical events and asked to interpret them in metaphoric ways. So the guillotine can be redefined as a symbol of love not death, and death the passage to another state as natural as that of life. This, by implication, asks us to seek hitherto unconsidered meanings for other known historical events and characters, meanings that it becomes our own business to discover.

Georges Danton and Georg Büchner

One of the commonest statements about *Danton* is that Büchner is, more or less, Danton. This is nonsense. They certainly are often close, a closeness that begins with their shared first names.[8] But Büchner put something of himself into every character, and there are few in the whole play who do not speak words traceable in similar forms in his letters and philosophy. Rather one should see the choice of *Danton* in terms more familiar from the Renaissance, as giving shape to a private battle in his own soul – a *psychomachia* – about the nature of politics, revolution and exile. In this battle Büchner distributes his own often contradictory impulses equally among the opponents and there is at the end certainly no outright winner.

There is however, pleasure in self-pity and self-dramatisation to which Büchner was not immune, a facet of his writing which reveals itself in quotation from or allusion to *Hamlet*. Büchner uses the soliloquy in a similar way to Shakespeare, allowing both Robespierre and Danton not just to provide information to the audience thereby but also treating the form as a private debate. Furthermore, Büchner, Danton and Hamlet all face exile or death, at least death of the will to act, and all three do not fully master the problem. The most famous soliloquy of all, 'To be or not to be', is a model for the one scene in the play with asides, where the young Laflotte is wondering whether to agree to denounce Danton in order to escape himself. Laflotte is young, highly strung, and oppressed by prisons, features he shares with Büchner:

> LAFLOTTE: (*aside*) He [Danton] is lost anyway. What does it matter then if I tread on a corpse to get out of the grave myself? [. . .] Well, of course it smells a bit of treachery [. . .] And then – I am not afraid of death, but of pain . . .' (3, 5)

The words recall the letter Büchner wrote on arriving in France after his flight from Darmstadt, but for all their personal honesty they are inconsistent: if Danton were the victim of natural law, he would need no denouncer. Why then does Büchner have Laflotte suggest that natural law needs human help?

While Büchner's response to stress invests the reactions of Danton, Camille and Laflotte, his intellectual energy is more obviously given to Danton's opponents, Robespierre and St Just:

> ROBESPIERRE: The social revolution is not yet finished; the man who completes only half a revolution digs his own grave. The upper class is not yet destroyed and the healthy strength of the common people must place itself in the role of this in every way debilitated class. Vice must be punished and morality must rule through terror. (1,6)

Despite the last sentence, Büchner certainly shared Robespierre's (and later Marx's) belief that the common people must replace the debilitated aristocracy, and he develops this theme further in his next play. He also stands squarely behind St Just's word, later in the play, in a speech departing substantially from the historical source:

> ST JUST: And so I ask: should moral nature show any more delicacy in her revolutions than physical nature? Cannot an idea destroy anything that opposes it just as well as a law of phsyics?' (2, 7)

It was an intrinsic part of advanced intellectual thinking of the day that ideas could have such an effect, and in Büchner's scientific work, written *after Danton*, it is clear that he shared St Just's opinion, hoping that his own writing would contribute to the success of the new idea of nature:

> Nature does not work according to design, she does not worry herself sick with an endless row of necessities, all of which are interdependent: she is rather in every manifestation directly *sufficient unto herself*. Everything that exists exists solely of its own accord.[9]

Büchner was more fatalistic than he implies through St Just as he did not believe that one could control the great idea once formulated and released into men's consciousness. This point he makes ironically; St Just prophesies his own death in terms that suggest that the idea of the Revolution has got beyond anyone's control:

> ST JUST: The Revolution is like the daughters of Pelias; she cuts mankind up into bits to make it young again.
> (2, 7)

In personal terms Büchner, in writing the play, cut his mind up into little bits in a still immature state and reconstituted it mature. But he was dogged in the process by the awareness that for Danton such intense self-criticism was ultimately self-destructive and, more seriously still, that all the Revolution itself had achieved was apparently the return of a revitalised ancien regime.

Staging

Danton remained unperformed until 1902, when the *Freie Volksbühne* staged it in Berlin: since then it has seldom been out of the repertoire except for a time during the early part of the Hitler government. Once it had been rediscovered its biggest problem was directors who did not think it would work on stage as it stood.

First the practicalities: *Danton* has, or rather can have, a huge cast, a vast and expensive variety of sets and makes consequent demands on the stage staff. This has tended to mean that big theatres and big production budgets have won the day over more modest endeavours, with a distinct emphasis on size for its own sake. There is also only one major part, Danton, and directors have tended to 'improve' the more minor roles to give their other principals adequate stage time. Only slowly have these tendencies been questioned.

Danton's history on stage reveals a split in attitudes between the majority of productions which have wished to portray the whole Revolution and a minority which have made the play a study of Danton in private. Yet the work actually needs a balanced use of both. Not surprisingly it was the epic scale of the play which dominated the attention of early directors many of whom were schooled in the 'epic' techniques of Brecht and Piscator. The play does deal with historical issues in an often didactic manner, it constantly interrupts the 'action', though not quite in the Brechtian style, and it can be acted in such a way that no sympathetic relationship is required between actors and audience. But simply because the play is epic in scope should not lead to such a simple equation with 'epic' theatre. It is not just, nor simply a study of class warfare; it 'sidetracks' into sexuality and individual concerns; and worst of all it breaks the prime Socialist Realist rule that the working class hero should be presented in an optimistic manner. But all too often on stage Danton's musings are drowned by the roars of the proletariat in revolt.

Historically speaking the grandiose approach was initially necessary to win audience enthusiasm and excitement. The play was presented as a long dance of death in celebration of the guillotine in which its infernal embrace really does become like the clasp of a woman's thighs, as at one point Danton suggests. And it was the greatest of this style of production which catapulted the work to fame and set the tone of the countless stagings that followed in the next twenty years. In December 1916, mid-way through the First World War, Max Reinhardt opened the play at the *Grosses Schauspielhaus* in Berlin, a huge theatre that by its size dictated a large-scale performance. He portrayed the Revolution in its full extent, using both stage and auditorium packed with people. Danton seemed to be on trial from the very start with the theatre audience being cast both as impartial jury and committed participants in the revolutionary fervour. Hans Mayer attributes the success of this production to the current war.[10] Everyone has to decide for himself whether to obey orders and what those orders mean. Everyone is caught up in an attack on an authoritarian state, because, Mayer argues, the play exposes the hypocrisy of those orders issued in the name of a people whose opinion was never asked.

Where the First World War liberated the political aspect of *Danton*, the Second exposed its poetic sub-text. Two productions from the 1950's in bomb-shattered Germany make this clear: no longer was the play seen as an incitement to revolt, but rather a warning against it. Max Geisenheyner reviewed a production in Mainz on 10 February 1955, praising Danton the poet over Robespierre the idealist:

And so Robespierre stands confronted by Danton: the ideological, unshakeable principle against the personal vitality and unique existence of the individual, who is aware of being bound in with the whole of human society but to whom the state as such is merely the administrative centre that is kept constantly under control of the commonwealth.[11]

The critic talks little about the production, but much about Danton: and behind Danton lies the memory of a different, more recent, bloody ideology, that of Nazism. Geysenheyner does so consciously, stating quite rightly that *Danton* is a play about types of conflict that become relevant to any society in conflict. (It was, strangely, performed in Berlin in 1939 in the hope its sentiments would fire Germans to follow the Führer.)

In September 1957 the distinguished local critic Georg Hensel reviewed a production in Büchner's Darmstadt. 'The decisive scenes in the play are the quiet ones, that deal with the decline of Danton, not a decline caused by the Revolution, nor by the intrigues of his opponents, but by his own changed relationship with the Revolution, with the world altogether . . . .'[12] Although Hensel is right to stress

81

the poetic scenes it is nevertheless striking that still in the 1950s no productive balance had been found between the play's 'poetry' and its 'revolution'.

Although Reinhardt set the tone for an apparently documentary, naturalistic style, his use of a largely abstract set always suggested a poetic tension just below the surface. The English, by contrast, confuse naturalism with literalism and a pedantic concern for authenticity. To this end both James Maxwell for the 1959 production at the Lyric, Hammersmith, (subsequently published by Methuen) and Stuart Griffith and Alan Clark for the BBC in April 1978, rewrote the text, allegedly to make it more accessible and more plausible. First Maxwell:

> And I have helped with the history. One would have to know one's French Revolution really well to cope with Büchner's play as it stands. So I have explained, altered or ignored many of the characters' references to the current affairs of the Revolution. All my editing was based on the wish that [. . .] this specially inspired, daring, and sympathetic vision of our humanity in its most destructive condition might be seen to happen more powerfully on the stage.

There are times as a critic when one rubs one's eyes in disbelief: what does 'help' with the history mean? Does one need to have read Mommsen and the *Cambridge Ancient History* to understand *Julius Caesar*? What kind of history is *King Lear*? Mr Maxwell rearranges scenes, destroying effectively the original structure and makes the act and scene arrangement into an episodic one. Taking as starting point the fact that Büchner was really Brecht he writes a new, inferior play with Büchner as source.

The key to his thinking lies in another heretical chestnut:

'It is significant that on television, where it is possible to edit separately shot scenes into unbroken continuity, the play was very successful indeed, more so than on stage.' Yet the smoothing hand of the editor is just what *Danton* does not need, as the BBC proved conclusively in April 1978.[13] Here the play opens not in the casino but with a highlight from Robespierre's speech to the Jacobin club – rather like showing the goals first on the evening football show. The rest comes later. The essential first impression therefore, of whores, gambling and death is lost in a piece of meaningless polemic that pushes the play into just the Hegelian battle of World Historical figures that it is not. To the same end, Lucile's final cry 'Long live the king' is cut and so the classically Büchnerian closing shift of perspective lost. Here and there, lest we lose interest, the Marseillaise is faded in, and with it all the technical tricks that television can play. The Büchner who is credited with discovering documentary theatre is also saddled with inventing the shooting script and who better than the *Forsyte Saga*'s makers to do justice to him? But this is to make Danton the literal historical leader that Büchner deliberately avoids. Danton is not like Shakespeare's Antony seen through moral spectacles, the ruler of a nation who is brought to his fall by booze and women, but a man who grows into an intellectual perception that death is the natural consequence of his life; a man who starts like Hamlet, paralysed by his own thought and then uses his awareness of that paralysis to penetrate a new mystery, that of nature.

This process is most crucially evident in two scenes, on which the success of a production stands or falls: the one is Danton's escape to the field (2, 4), the other a crowd scene (3, 10). Before he is seen in the field Danton announces that he is going for a walk, and when we next see him he is out of Paris. It would be very hard indeed to make this abrupt transition work naturalistically, which indicates that the walk is not to be taken in this way. When Danton walks into the country it is not romantic nature, daffodils and lakes, that he sees but himself: it is quiet and he is threatened by the sound of his footsteps, a sound which is hardly likely to be naturalistic, as footfall on grass is generally silent, as it is on the earth. He sits down, not because he is tired or has blisters, but because the noise stops when he does. This noise reminds him terribly of a whole world he has forgotten, where the individual matters. Sat on the thin crust of the earth, through which Woyzeck later hears voices, it is life, love, memory, death which pierce his consciousness not blood or politics and Danton realises that his memory has sucked him in and what he has been is now more real to those around him than what he is. He cannot kill himself, not because he fears the sleep of death, but because that will only further freeze the false memory others have of him in a state he now rejects. The parallel the scene suggests is Dives and Lazarus, for Danton realises, like Dives, that hell is the persistent memory of injustice. It is not Lazarus or God who keeps Dives in hell, but Dives himself.

The stage directions of the scene ask for two distinct gestures and one silence. Danton sits down and is silent. It is a silence that could be eternal, and is the only such in the play: in his decision to break that silence Danton apparently denies negation and nihilism, and after a while he gets up and goes back to Paris. It is tempting to see in this a classic moral *peripeteia*, a reversal of attitude; but we learn at the close of the scene that the threat of the silence was suppressed not broken by his words. It was less Macbeth turning to fight than Lear, or Lenz, stilling the rising storm; and indeed in the very next scene this storm breaks over Danton. All his haunting memories crowd back as he looks

1a. *Georg Büchner,* penned sketch by Alexis Muston, from Fischer, *Georg Büchner Untersuchungen und Marginalien* (Bonn: Bouvier Verlag Herbert Grundmann, 1972) by kind permission Professor Fischer

1b. *Georg Büchner,* an engraving by Auerbach, original by Adolf Hoffmann

2a. Albert Steinrück as Woyzeck in the première of *Woyzeck* at the Residenztheater, Munich, 8 November 1913 directed by Eugen Kilian, Theater Museum Munich

2b. Bruno Decarli as Robespierre in *Danton's Death*, Grosses Schauspielhaus Berlin, 1916, directed by Max Reinhardt, Theater Museum Munich

3. The guillotine scene from *Danton's Death*, Darmstadt 1957, directed by G. R. Sellner, designed by Franz Mertz

4.   Max Noack as Robespierre (*l.*), Fred Tanner (*c.*) as Danton, and A. M. Rueffer as St Just (*r.*) in *Danton's Death,* Darmstadt 1957. Photograph: Pit Ludwig

5. Claus Eberth (c.) as Danton in *Danton's Death*, Kammerspiele Munich 1980, directed by Dieter Dorn. The waxwork group (l.) represents Danton, La Marseillaise and Robespierre. Photograph: Rabanus

6.   Albrecht Peter as Wozzeck and Elisabeth Lindermeier as Marie in
     Wozzeck, the opera by Alban Berg, Prinzregententheater Munich 1957,
     conducted by Ferenc Fricsay, directed by Rudolf Hartmann, designed
     by Helmut Jürgens. Photograph: Sabine Toepffer

7.   Diego Leon as President, Wolfram Mehring as Leonce and Grillon as Valerio in *Leonce and Lena*, directed by Wolfram Mehring, Théâtre Franco-Allemand, Paris 1959. Photograph: Etienne Weill

8. The Gate Theatre production of *Leonce and Lena*, London 1980, directed by Nick Hamm

out of the window into the night.

The silence in the field between sitting down and getting up is the mid-point of the plot and at the same time the decisive intervention of another world, the silent, into the world of words that Danton inhabits. This silence reveals that what binds the scenes together is not slick editing but ever richer silence. The two directions set either side of it ask Danton simply to sit down and to get up, but what a world of meaning there is in both.

In direct contrast to this 'orientation' scene where the view from the field acts as an Archimedean vantage point from which to contemplate the Revolution, is the crowd scene, reminiscent of that moment in *Julius Caesar* when Mark Antony releases the frenzied Romans from his spell:

SEVERAL WOMEN: The guillotine is a bad mill, and Samson a poor baker's boy; we want bread, bread!
(3, 10)

The women's message is the same as the *Courier's* that no Revolution has any point unless it feeds the starving – the 'bread question' which caused the student Büchner to reject all other revolutionary movements than his own since they were well-fed and middle-class. He saw that hunger was brutalising the Hessian peasant, that the Parisian mob was brutalised first by hunger and only then by blood. Robespierre has no bread so he offers the blood of others; Danton has no bread so he goes to the guillotine to offer his own blood. To make the point more chilling a woman presses her children through the crowd to watch his execution to take their minds off their empty stomachs: probably the village women in Kampuchea did the same.

The counterpoint of bread and blood opens up the most difficult area of the play, the religious and sacramental.

Bread and blood appear together in the final scenes to suggest a messianic side to Danton, dying to save his country with his blood. Perhaps Büchner had fantasies of this kind. But he knew in his heart, as did Danton that this allusion was false, that blood is shed *en masse* but it brings neither bread nor deliverance. All it does is confront the leaders with bodily needs and make basic living standards a higher priority than well-learned dogma. When Danton thinks of the body he is not solely sensual, nor even primarily motivated by the pleasures of touch but because he knows that if his people do not have enough to eat and drink, clothes on their backs and roofs over their heads no ideal on earth will make them better off. This challenges Christianity outright: if history is God's will, how could God will the Terror? If God did will the Terror then it is our duty to fight Him, to free ourselves from Him as only then will we direct our efforts to improving the human condition on earth rather than speculatively storing up for ourselves treasure in heaven.

Set against the two massive forces of bread and silence, exactly who Danton is and what was his part in which revolution is of secondary importance. It does not matter greatly if he dies on the scaffold or is 'dead' before the play starts: it is essential only that the play works as a single, continuous whole – a *gestus* – an immediately recognisable and unfalsifiable metaphor of the immutable laws of nature. It must convince its audience that Danton's death must have felt like that, however it actually was. That Büchner personally felt it deeply is clear from these two passages:

JULIE: You rescued the country.

DANTON: Yes, I did. That was self-defence, we had to. The man on the cross had it easy: 'It must be that offences come, but woe unto him by whom the offence cometh.' It must, that was this must. Who will curse the hand on whom the curse of 'must' has fallen? Who has spoken this 'must', who? What is it in us that whores, lies, steals and murders? We are puppets, pulled on strings by unknown forces; nothing, we ourselves are nothing. (2, 5)

In the letter he wrote to Minna early in 1834 about the 'fatalism of history' we read the same thing:

The individual is merely foam on a wave, greatness mere accident, the rule of genius is puppetry, a ridiculous wrestling with an iron law in which the greatest achievement is simply to become aware of it, to overcome it is impossible. [...] I accustomed my eye to blood. But I am not the guillotine blade. *Must* is one of those words of damnation with which men are christened. The verse: 'It must needs be that offences come but woe unto him by whom the offence cometh' is appalling. What is it in us that lies, murders and steals?[14]

Once again Büchner shows he was not averse to self-dramatisation, but the fact that he and Danton say more or less the same thing does not mean that they are the same. Rather, he sees the fact that he and Danton reach the same conclusion as evidence for the existence of that great natural law that the philosopher Büchner had predicated. After all, Büchner lived on when Danton died, a conscious decision as his letter to Gutzkow accompanying his script showed: the 'must' operating on Büchner was not the same 'must' operating on Danton.

5
Leonce and Lena

More than any other of Büchner's works, *Leonce and Lena* has suffered from being put in the wrong critical box and then being criticised for not having the qualities of work in that box. The box in question is 'comedy', that is comedy in the wispish, romantic, ever-so-nice sense, comedy the way *A Midsummer Night's Dream* used to be thought comic, with lots of fairies in trailing, transparent chiffon and delicate asses heads, more flowers than ass. It was perhaps Bottom's orgasm in Peter Brook's famous production that liberated that play world-wide from at least some of its sentimentality and made of it the play of light and dark, and more dark than light, that it is. *Leonce and Lena* in the English-speaking world needs something like this orgasm to shake it free of terms like 'a collector's piece' of 'theatrical curiosity' that even in London in 1980 typify the way the work is seen. Still harder to grasp is the comment, again from a London critic, that the play is 'weak'. For a weak play it has caused more than its share of upsets, not least in Prague and East Berlin in the last decade where it has been closed down by the authorities.

Of all critics it is surely Hans Mayer, again, who got the work right when he said that the basic urge in it is hatred, hatred of a political system it parodies, hatred of an intellectual movement it thoroughly undermines.[1] This hatred is most visible in the scene (3, 2) in front of the castle when the hungry peasants, hitherto suppressed in the play, are allowed to *smell* roasting meat for the first time in their lives, though certainly not to eat any. But it also underlies the portrait of King Peter, who, it must be remembered is a king, and the apparent failure of Prince Leonce to undertake any steps to change the world he takes over from his father, the least excusable failure of all. Far from Büchner moving away from politics, as is often claimed of this play, he is merely diversifying his tactics.[2] While it is not my purpose to deny the play is funny, the real question the laughter raises is who is laughing at whom, and in what tone?

Almost exactly one year after the completion of *Danton*, Büchner read of a prize offered by the Stuttgart publisher and book-seller, J. G. Cotta, for 'the best one or two act comedy in prose or verse.' As well as 300 guilders in prize money the winner would have his play printed in Lewald's *Theatre Review* of that year. The closing date was 1 July, later extended by two months. Nevertheless, Büchner was late in handing in his entry and it was returned unread. As the most authoritative date of composition is April and May of that year,[3] 1836, it is odd, to say the least, that Büchner should have been so late, the more so as *Danton* proved he could work at great speed and *Leonce* is only half *Danton's* length. His self-confidence was high, and, judging from his output, he was in no way suffering from a block. Nor, despite being cut off from his father, was he financially desperate, much though he would have appreciated 300 guilders.

As with *Danton* the artistic impulses for writing lie in the interaction between his long-term reading and his immediate personal situation. From the beginning of his education Büchner had been widely versed in new German literature, especially the romantics of whom his mother was so fond. But after the *Courier* affair Büchner suddenly found their particular ideals and enthusiasms wholly inappropriate to the political and social needs of the day. Some of this dissatisfaction we have seen reflected in *Lenz*, written at about the same time. In *Leonce and Lena* he takes on effectively a whole romantic generation, parodying its style, manners and attitudes. To this he added the anger which he felt over the fate of Lenz, to whom Leonce, as his name suggests, is an ironic foil; Leonce has Lenz's *Weltschmerz* but lacks his humanity; Leonce runs away like Lenz, but for selfish not societal reasons.

The immediate constraint on Büchner however, was to avoid trouble with the Strasbourg authorities who knew both of the *Courier* and *Danton*. If he were to continue to write he would have to avoid political controversy, or risk deportation. In these terms *Lenz* was 'safe' since it was a quiet, personal study – at least to the official eye. But for all Büchner's restraint in *Leonce and Lena* he found he could not represent a kingdom without showing the peasants in it and although he restricts them to one appearance, that very restriction made the political aspect of the work more powerful. This implies that his main reason for being late with the play was constant fear of the consequences were it to be published. In September he did finally send the manuscript off to Cotta *after* he had been given his post in Zürich and a certificate of good conduct from the Strasbourg police, a document he required having left with no passport from Darmstadt. How different our reaction to the play would be had it caused his deportation from Strasbourg: yet it is a profoundly political work. War does not have to be fought with guns, and while *Leonce* is no agitation and propaganda play it is committed to the same principles as the *Courier* and the Society for the Rights of Man.

Plot: Form as meaning

Büchner's contemporary, Hebbel, himself a dramatist, wrote that 'Form is the highest content'. Form in *Leonce* is as significant as in *Danton* but harder to describe since the play has two apparently contradictory formal impulses in it, which, on the surface at least, cause considerable turbulence. There is a romantic comedy about a young, handsome prince who runs away from court, falls in love, marries and lives happily ever after, a witty parody of Clemens Brentano's *Ponce de Leon*. There is also a picaresque 'educational' plot, worked in episodes not scenes, about a bored young prince being introduced for the first time to real feeling, a formal pattern and purpose that derives directly from Laurence Sterne. Leonce even refers explicitly to *Tristram Shandy*.[4] The narrative strategies Büchner takes over from Sterne are a deliberately confused sense of time and place and a self-conscious attitude to fictionalisation: this resolves itself into a classic 'cock and bull' tale, that as a tale has led nowhere. Using Sterne as model, Büchner subverts his romantic comedy with picaresque intrusions which increasingly determine the plot structure. Act 1 is built like a classic comic exposition and is nearly as long as the other two acts together: yet Acts 2 and 3 have each as many scenes as Act 1, all but the last of which are very short and only loosely related. At the outset we seem to be offered a story of boredom, anticipating Chekhov in its naturalism, only to shift into a surreal picaresque mode in Act 2.

The one continuous thread is the education of the young prince, which we are shown, quasi-novelistically, mostly through his own eyes. As his sense of himself changes, most noticeably at the end of Act 1, so the discourse changes with him. This technique is deliberately deceptive, just as is Sterne's. While at first we seem to be invited to accept Leonce's values as they stand, the play makes it steadily harder for us to do so, until in the closing moments Leonce, in the last of the many revelations, is shown to be yet one more totalitarian despot. The educative process through which Leonce has been taken has led him nowhere: but the audience has subtly been shown how insidiously easy it is for totally reprehensible social and political attitudes to establish themselves in a society. Nowhere is Büchner's political bitterness clearer than in this: Leonce stands for all the young men of the post-1789 world, excited by the changes of 1793 and even 1814. While his father, Peter, could be forgiven for not wanting change, born as he was into a pre-revolutionary world, for Leonce there is no excuse. But how, wonders Büchner, can a man born with the same body and brain as a peasant slowly come to believe he is somehow different, privileged? How can his education so destroy the nature with which he was born? The process by which Büchner draws us into Leonce's mind and shows us its bigotry is both the form and meaning of his play. How, then, is it done?

Prince Leonce of the kingdom of Popo (literally, the baby word for a child's bottom) is due to marry the daughter of the king of Pipi (literally, the same as English wee-wee, a child's urine) whom he has never met. Leonce is caught in a Hamlet-like melancholy, however, and quotes *Hamlet* to prove it. Surrounded by courtiers as playing-cards like those in Alice's Wonderland he finds relief only in the sort of senseless mind-teasers that characterised the excesses of romantic, speculative philosophy. How, for example, can one see the top of one's own head? His condition he describes as *Müßiggang* – the choice of word is his – the least translateable but most central of all romantic terms. That Büchner establishes *Müßiggang* for him, (he is actually sprawled out on a bench spitting at a stone no less than 365 times) should make us suspicious that what Leonce intends by it and what Büchner himself believes are poles apart. How does Leonce see *Müßiggang*? The classic definition of the term is to be found in Friedrich Schlegel's novel *Lucinde* which Leonce surely has read avidly:

> O *Müßiggang, Müßiggang:* you are the breath of life, of innocence and of enthusiasm! You are the breath of life to the blessed and he is blessed who has and who cherishes you, you holy jewel. The one fragment of similarity with God that was left to us from paradise.[5]

One cannot believe that Büchner thinks Leonce's *Müßiggang* has any sincerity in it, for all its willing imitation of the melancholic *ennui* which enriches the pages of *Lucinde*. As so often the context says all: this is a prince, soon to be king, talking, as mindless of his responsibilities to himself and his court as to his people in the country. This is the Grand Duke Ludwig II of Hessen speaking, who saw no contradiction in a starving population and a private orchestra of 85 players for his own amusement. To compound the irony, Büchner then puts a speech almost identical to one he gives Lenz into Leonce's mouth, once again using the context to completely reverse the meaning conveyed: everything men do, claims Leonce, stems from *Müßiggang* and they do it to ward off the boredom that would otherwise engulf them. But while the *Müßiggang*, the lost sense of paradise, is something Lenz genuinely seeks in the Vosges mountains,

Leonce's boredom is nothing more than the inevitable state of a mind with nothing to strive for.

Leonce's boredom does have deep and serious causes, as Büchner knew from his own experience, and as he could read in Alfred de Musset's *Fantasio*, which had a direct influence on *Leonce*, and *Confession d'un enfant du siècle*. 'The whole sickness of the present age,' wrote Musset, 'stems from two causes. The people who experienced 1793 and 1814 [one might add 1830] carry two wounds in their hearts. Everything that once was is no longer; everything that is still to come does not yet exist.' While Musset's diagnosis suggests that Leonce's condition is less his personal fault than the malaise of an age, the ailment he describes certainly affected Büchner, and it gives *Leonce* a strangely *fin de siècle* feeling. Perhaps if one imagines what Oscar Wilde might have done with the plot of *The Importance of Being Earnest* after his stay in Reading gaol one can gauge how 'comedy' was not the first thought in Büchner's mind with *Leonce*.

Musset's observations work themselves out in the plot. Leonce's youth and his love for Rosetta are past – Hamlet has abandoned Ophelia – but no revenge or other motive is in sight to alleviate the emptiness that this farewell to youth has caused. The only way out is to run away from responsibility and marriage. Here again, the structure has its own message: the decision to escape is taken actually half-way through the play although in classical terms it is where the plot truly begins. For Büchner more important than the boredom, or the love affair was the portrayal of the state of Popo. Each of the three expository scenes in Act 1 shows us a different aspect of this kingdom, set in polemical contrast: first the mind of the heir apparent; next, the king himself; and last the decadence of the society in which both live.

Leonce's *Müßiggang* I have already discussed, but if the

context itself is not enough to expose its fraudulence, the arrival of the court fool, Valerio, certainly does. Like Touchstone and Toby Belch in one, Valerio is a drunkard and wit, but with a steady eye to his own main chance. He it is who makes the first, penetrating observations about political matters, comparing himself (like Hamlet) cynically with Alexander the Great:

> Ha! I am Alexander the Great! How the sun shines me a golden crown in my hair! How my uniform sparkles![6]

His uniform is no less than the jester's motley but as his remarks remind us the fool belongs with the king. The irony is that they have in fact changed places and Valerio emerges at the end of the play with all the real power.

Only after the parody of power and Valerio's jokes about the royal preoccupations with the army, the treasury, the mistress and the heir comes the real thing, King Peter: and Peter is a parody of the parody. He fancies himself a philosopher-king and even while he is dressing finds time to muse on the world. As he looks down at his unbuttoned clothes he cries: 'Stop! My God! My free will down the front there is completely exposed, where are my cuffs?'[7] The coalescence in his mind of the real world of cuffs with the speculative concerns of free will is grotesque enough in itself, but when the sexual undertones of 'free will' are added, with their echoes of Lear's Fool in the storm, the king's monomania becomes frighteningly deranged. This king worries at even having to see his Privy Council, let alone his people: this nervousness and fear are fused in the emblem of the knot he has tied in his handkerchief, the meaning of which he has now forgotten. The knot, quite simply, is the people! Yet in forgetting, Peter illustrates once again Musset's point: as a ruler who has lost touch with those he rules he is a sign that is no longer in any meaningful relation with what it signifies. Just how catastrophic this has become is shown when he finally enters the council chamber only to close the meeting immediately because he cannot remember its purpose. The scene's wit is close in strategy to Chaplin's in the *Great Dictator* – which also depends heavily on background knowledge for its political satire to work – as, for instance, in the shaving scene between Hitler and Mussolini. Both Chaplin and Büchner attempt, in their respective ways, to achieve by wit what no preaching could.

Seen against Peter's monomania, Leonce's behaviour in the next scene becomes less and less funny. It is set in a room as opulent as anything out of the *Count of Monte Cristo*. Büchner exploits the internal contradiction between the words and the setting, but also, later, between this opulence and the poverty that makes it possible. Leonce closes out the day and surrounds himself with artificial, and hence unnatural night. He is joined by Rosetta, his former mistress – one hesitates to say love – and their talk turns on three themes, boredom, time and love. As in *Danton* the link between the three is death.

First boredom:

ROSETTA: So you love me out of sheer boredom?
LEONCE: On the contrary, I am bored because I love you. But I love being bored as much as I love you. You are one and the same thing.[8]

The coalition of love with boredom is complete, demanding either the removal of one of the two words from the lexicon or its redefinition. The proposition that language sets the boundaries of the perceivable world, a highly 'modern' notion, is here anticipated in a highly egocentric discourse whose meanings are determined solely by the experience of the user. For Leonce, love and boredom are the same experiences and so he equates the two verbally, which is all very witty but princes in countries like Popo can redefine words like 'Jew' and 'state security' in ways far less funny.

Next time makes an appearance, clashing seemingly prosaically with the 'poetic' mood:

ROSETTA: You love me, Leonce?

LEONCE: Ah! Why not?

ROSETTA: For ever?

LEONCE: Oh! That's a long word, forever. If I love you for five thousand years and seven months more, is that enough? I agree it's a lot less than for ever, but it's still a fair amount of time: and we can take our time loving one another.

ROSETTA: But time might take our loving from us.

LEONCE: Or loving may make the time seem short.[9]

Leonce's hard-headed sums contrast with Rosetta's vision of eternity in a way that suggest a break from romantic day-dreaming; through the contrast a temporal relativity is established that is familiar to us all – that hours in love are short and in pain are long. But we must not allow this relativity to stop us acting to help ourselves now, which, for all his escape, Leonce never really does. The fact that history seems to be moving at his own pace, with or without us, does not mean a licence for fatalism as even passivity can be a form of action.

In one respect, Leonce does progress and this emerges from his speech to Rosetta about the death of his love. Rosetta tries to embrace him:

LEONCE: Careful! My head! I have laid our love to rest
there. Look through the windows of my eyes. Don't
you see how prettily dead the poor thing is? Can't you
see the two white roses on its cheeks and the two red
roses on its breast? Don't touch me lest I break a little
arm off: that would be too sad. I must take care to
keep my head absolutely straight on my shoulders,
like a wailing woman with a child's coffin.[10]

Büchner takes the grave images from *Danton* and the essay
on Descartes a step further, in the direction of surrealism.
But there is also a departure from *Danton*: Danton sees his
love as buried inside Julie's lap, but Leonce thinks of his as
buried in his own head. Where Danton fears his memory
and tries to relieve his feelings of grief by unburdening
them on someone else, Leonce understands how he can use
memory to cope with grief internally without fearing for his
own stability. The memory has a new, positive function, in
that it allows the individual to 'archive' old emotions and so
release space in the front of the mind for new develop-
ments. Danton's obsessive concern with his past prevents
his continuing growth either privately or politically. Leonce
is freed of any such obsession in rejecting Rosetta, and can,
in theory, now develop.

There are both dangers and difficulties attendant on the
process of forgetting. All too easily Leonce learns to use his
memory as a kind of mask to his self, forgetting real feelings
almost as soon as he has experienced them. He finds too,
that immediately after he has erased those feelings from his
mind the result is not joy but emptiness:

LEONCE: 'My life yawns at me, like a huge white sheet of
paper that I'm supposed to fill and cannot mark with a
single letter. My head is like an empty dance floor

[. . .] the last dancers have taken their masks off and now look one another straight in the eye, dead tired [. . .] I know myself so well that I can say what I shall be doing and dreaming in fifteen minutes, a week, a year.[11]

The speech is set in inverted commas – Leonce is acting Leonce (or Hamlet). He announces a new start, as if in articulating his grief he is accepting it. It is also the moment in the play when Büchner shifts the focus of his attention from the ostensible plot about young lovers to the metaphors of unmasking, death and cracked instruments, which then dominate. To underline the point, the Privy Council next enters, bringing in the daylight, to find Leonce sitting on the ground, just as Danton had done in the field outside Paris. For a moment there is the possibility that Leonce is about to face his responsibilities, but the moment is brief. Rather than using his new awareness to tackle the problems of his court, he decides to run away, not to war, nor to write but to beg.

This last remark can be thrown away by the actor, a plan no more serious than Bob Hope and Bing Crosby off to Morocco. But if he views it in the light of the play's epigraph from Alfieri '*E la fame*?' – 'what of hunger?' – and '*E la fama*?' – 'What of fame?' – how to deliver the line becomes one of the most difficult decisions of the whole part. What if Leonce is serious and, for all his jokiness, (and there is no psychological implausibility in that) does care about hunger? Or what if he has never thought seriously about hunger at all and is heartlessly flippant? Hunger confronts both Leonce and Büchner, though in different ways. It challenges Leonce to work for the reform of Popo, a challenge he fails to meet. It challenged Büchner to say what use was poetry when the masses were starving. Was writing a betrayal of the peasant cause? Was the consolation of Weidig's religion, that man cannot live by bread alone, a cruel sop for men who had no bread? In the West with our shops full of food, hunger rarely touches us personally: but Büchner saw that it would be the decisive issue for mankind.

After a brief scene to introduce Lena (perhaps notable for its lack of any hint of criticism of the role she has to play in a male-ordered world) Büchner effects a typical switch of environment to a rustic inn. Here the future lovers, running away like Oedipus from what they think to be their destiny, actually encounter it where they think themselves safe. The setting for the discovery, for all its bucolic delights, has for Leonce the claustrophobic atmosphere of a tiny hall of mirrors. Sun, time and space all play tricks, which the earthy naturalism of the inn accentuates:

> VALERIO: (*breathing heavily*) Upon my word, Prince, the world is, I must say, like a huge sprawling building.

> LEONCE: Not in the least! I hardly dare stretch out my arms, like in a tiny hall of mirrors, for fear I bang into everything, smash the pretty figures and they would lie in splinters around my feet, with nothing but cold, bare walls before my eyes.[13]

The differences between the two perceptions are crucial to the play's strategy of contrast: firstly Valerio is breathing heavily whereas Leonce is not, something we see on stage before either speaks. They both use architectural images to describe what they feel, suggesting neither of these courtiers is prepared to admit of a natural explanation of the world. They differ however, in that Valerio sees wide prospects where Leonce fears to reach out. Their disagreement is analogous to Leonce's earlier exchange with Rosetta on the nature of time and recalls the debate in the essay on Cartesius between fixed and relative views of the connection between space and matter. Add to this the further dimension of the relativity of time and one is on ground more familiar as Einstein's.

The relativity of perception operates in the intellectual as well as the physical universe, as becomes clear in Leonce's description of his ideal woman:

> Deep within my heart there lies my ideal woman and I must seek her out. She is perfectly beautiful and perfectly mindless.[14]

The philosophical joke embedded in the remark is that perfection actually means imperfection – either you are perfectly beautiful and stupid, or vice versa. The joke's expense is not at womanhood but at metaphysics. Its point is made clear from Lena who is both beautiful and clever. The fusion of opposites, as Leonce presents them to us, is probably the single most positive aspect to the play for she personifies a nature that actually refuses man-made relativities and simply is. She states that true nature has only one, unfalsifiable shape and that shape is, *de facto*, lovely.

Lena's lovely naturalness is reinforced by a different natural image, that of the onion (an image also used in T. S. Eliot's *Murder in the Cathedral*):

> VALERIO: Damn it! Here's another border already. This country is like an onion, nothing but layers, or like Chinese boxes; in the biggest box is nothing but boxes and in the smallest box is nothing at all.[15]

The metaphor works not solely on a political level, criticising the absurd structure of a Germany divided into so many ineffectual units, but also ridicules that aspect of metaphysics which follows a line of speculation to the point when it disappears into nothing. Seen in its picaresque mode, the metaphor has a positive aspect; in the course of even a short journey the perceptive traveller may cross an infinite set of boundaries or thresholds of the mind. This sentiment derives from Sterne who points out through the metaphor of a journey, which has about it both the linear sense of crossing boundaries but also the spiritual sense of going deeper into the self, that it is more the act of travelling than the goal which gives the journey its value. It is not worth worrying whether the physical world is big or small, but it is of great value to live in that world, for if one thinks only of the end of the journey one will suddenly be surprised to find that that end is none other than death.

No sooner have Leonce and Valerio gone into the inn in pursuit of bodily refreshment than the complementary half of the scene is played by Lena and the governess. They, too, experience time in relative ways:

> GOVERNESS: There must be a spell on the day, the sun won't set and it's an eternity since we ran away.
> LENA: That can't be true, darling, I picked these flowers as we left the garden on our departure and they are hardly wilted at all.[16]

Once again the contrasts are abundant. The governess feels she has been walking for ever and Lena as if she had just left home: yet that the flowers are still fresh seems to be an objective indicator that Lena is right. But are the flowers to be taken naturalistically? If they are genuine and fresh, the two obviously cannot have been walking for long. If, however, the freshness is taken metaphorically they suggest both Lena's naturalness and eternal freshness of nature, oddly out of place in this man-made world. Matters are complicated still further by the governess observing that it is now nearly night! Time plays similar tricks in Shakespearian drama, but Büchner takes typically Shakespearian metaphoric properties of the night – transformation, confusion, death and magic – and applies them to the day, effectively answering in the affirmative Robespierre's question at the window whether day is not just a different kind of dream from night.

This day-night confusion spills over into the love between Leonce and Lena which begins in the twilight and ripens by moonlight. Even at the high point of his ecstasy at finding his perfect love Leonce's thoughts are on death, and he talks about the death-clock ticking in his chest when first he sees Lena. She responds to him by singing about the churchyard by moonshine, and he caps this by trying to jump into the river. These feelings resolve themselves into a single image, when Lena, *sitting on the ground* looks up at the moon above and compares it with a dead child, an image hauntingly similar to the use of the moon in Lorca's *Romancero Gitano*:

LEONCE: Arise in your white dress and follow the corpse
    through the night, singing it a requiem.
LENA: Who's there?
LEONCE: A dream.
LENA: Dreams are blessed.
LEONCE: Then dream yourself blessed and let me be
    your blessed dream.
LENA: The most blessed dream is death.
LEONCE: So let me be your angel of death then. Let my
    lips touch your eyes as softly as his wings.[17]

Few European writers have equalled Büchner's gift of combining death, love and sensuality so thrillingly and so chillingly as this: perhaps he even surprised himself on occasion at the fire of his own psyche, afraid and yet hypnotised by the Lenzian visions he had as he wrote. In this exchange the play completes its transformation from classical comedy to episodic fantasy.

Lena runs out, frightened by Leonce and by his intuitive grasp of her mood, a firm impression of him lodged in her mind but a weak one in her eyes since she can barely have seen his face. No love scene, courtship or marriage proposal follows, no explanation of why her escape ends. Leonce and Valerio discuss a wedding very perfunctorily, and Valerio agrees, on promise of high office to make the arrangements. When the lovers next appear together it is as large, humanoid puppets, programmed by Valerio – threateningly different from the fool we thought him to be – to perform certain actions, the first of which is to marry. Even when they are unmasked one wonders if they are still being 'worked' by a master puppeteer. Büchner is too good a writer to suppose that he abandoned the romantic love-story simply because it bored him, so what was he trying to do? Perhaps two things: firstly, anticipating *Woyzeck*, he was experimenting with how much of the 'story' you can leave out of a play and still take your audience with you. Having established a situation by the end of Act 1, in Act 2 he is more concerned with a quality of experience than what happens next. Secondly, he was examining some of the insidious ideological assumptions of clichés. The cliché is an obvious indicator of the values of a particular society or social group because the common currency of its meaning in itself is a mark of its widespread acceptability. One such cliché is the happy ending to the prince meets princess fairy tale, which rests both on the assumption that there should be privileged people and that their fate is especially interesting.[18] Büchner resisted these propositions and in his refusal of a happy ending and, specifically, in the puppet-show, an image with which he had condemned the Hessian court in the *Courier*, he again asks who pulls the strings of history and why.

The new answer is not a straightforward one, and borders on the self-contradictory. We see Valerio stripping off a potentially infinite series of masks. What these masks are, and whether the last mask is his face, we are not told, but suddenly the possibility arises that he was the true centre of the play all along, controlling those around him in a smilingly villainous way. There is, briefly, the hope that the result of all this unmasking will be a return to a natural selfhood, without falsity or pretension. But as the masks continue to fall it begins to dawn on us that the truth is hopelessly and irretrievably lost in Popo, that signs have lost touch with the signified. The one truth that can be extricated is that there is only multiplicity in this decadent world. Such a perception is in its way more radical even than the message of the *Courier* for it states that the empti-ness of the individual Leonce is the product of the empti-ness of the ruling class and so condemns that class in a manner now familiar from Marx. Valerio therefore takes on the role of great puppeteer of history with an unknown face, a parodic World Spirit, not unknown because he is like St Paul's unknown God in Corinth, but unknown because he has no face. Leonce and Lena are both human and puppet because the behaviour and attitudes they learn and practice at court are indistinguishable from the clock-work motions of mechanical dolls. The puppeteer does not himself know if he is really in control, so many masks does he wear. When boy gets girl nothing has really changed and their characters are so profoundly undermined that even if they think they have finished their charade, they certainly have not.

The conflict between Büchner's and Leonce's world views recurs in the final scene, one that is consistently misunderstood. The four leading figures remain on stage to talk of their ideal state. Leonce talks of a world where work is outlawed, where toys and theatre are his chief concerns and where time too is banished: the sun shines all day and the calendar measured by that same almanac of flowers that closes Marvell's *The Garden*. But it seems inconceivable that the man who was in political exile would have meant the closing words to be taken at their face value:

> VALERIO: And I shall be minister of state and it shall be decreed that all men who work blisters on their hands shall be arrested and all those who work themselves sick shall be treated as criminals and anyone who boasts he eats his bread buttered with the sweat of his brow shall be declared insane and a menace to society. Then we'll all lie down in the shade and pray God for macaroni, melons and figs, for musical larynxes, classical figures and a religion that knows its place.[19]

Büchner is rather himself putting on, or off, the last mask, in the manner of Grabbe's appearance in person at the end of *Scherz*, parodying the romantic idealists and scorning the sterility of the Big Rock Candy Mountain state which Valerio envisages. The total idiocy of a political future that does not take account of the present realities of states like Hessen, the need to feed and clothe the people – these are the real meanings of Valerio's speech. For this is a world where men have holes in their clothes, have never tasted meat, and where their ruler can make them stand in the sun all day only to be told to come back tomorrow to do the whole thing again.

This command is often overlooked, or laughed off, but if it is funny, it is a decidedly hellish sort of laughter. It grows quite naturally out of Leonce's musings on the endless repetition of moments in time and points once again to Büchner's own frustration at the way despots never seem to be able to break out of their own vicious circle of privilege. The moment is brutal and brief, not brutal because it is violent and bloody but because in a glimpse of hell, it fixes the true relationship between ruler and ruled:

> LEONCE: Go home now, but don't forget your speeches, sermons and poems because tomorrow, in our own good time, and with lots of fun, we're going to play the whole joke again from the beginning.[20]

No word here of the roast meat being given to the hungry for their trouble, no hint of a request. The command gives no hint that the peasants might have anything else to do. And who thinks the past day was a joke? Leonce does not say how much of the joke will be replayed, but there is no reason why we should not find him tomorrow sitting on a bench spitting at stones and rejecting Rosetta, or maybe Lena, all over again. It is as chilling a prospect as Vladimir and Estragon waiting tomorrow for Godot.

This Sysyphean vision of endless repetition is a direct challenge to both form and character in the classical sense since it denies both the special nature of the individual and the concept of an ending. Where Danton comes to rest in death, Leonce and the kingdom of Popo are condemned to permanently frustrated boredom. By this, Büchner places himself half-way between Sterne's and Sartre's views on time and existence, half-way between life as a meaningless cock-and-bull tale and hell. The chief character is the plot itself, or more accurately, the string of scenic metaphors set in counterpoint, and is essentially tragic for all the laughter, for that laughter, like Titus Andronicus's, is born of too many tears. Büchner's exile has robbed him of laughter of a frivolous kind. The utter insufficiency of Leonce's response to the realities of contemporary social and political needs is his own admission of defeat as a prince and king. It is also Büchner's most despairing attack on the Hessian ruling élite.

Staging

Two productions of this play not only demonstrate its strength on stage, if properly handled, but also the crucial importance of the puppet-peasant axis on which it rests. These are Wolfram Mehring's 1960 production in Paris and the 1978 *Volksbühne* production in East Berlin. The difficulties the work faces in countries not attuned to either puppetry or political theatre are exemplified by Nick Hamm's production at the Gate Theatre, London, in 1980 – in my own translation. These I shall deal with in turn. It is however, another of those ironies of Büchner history that the very first of his plays to be staged, by Max Halbe in a garden near the Munich north cemetery in 1895, should now be the least performed and least understood.

Wolfram Mehring's Théâtre Franco-Allemand production prefaces its programme with a short quotation from Gordon Craig: 'The "super-marionette" is the comedian with the most fire and the least egoism. With the sacred fire, the fire of the Gods and the fire of the devils but without the smoke and the steam humans put there.' This is supported by a series of related quotations which develop

Büchner's epigraph to Act 1, Touchstone's words from *As You Like It* 'Oh that I were a fool! I am enamoured of a motley coat.' Reflecting the depth of Craig's influence on Mehring's directorial concept, only Leonce is left un-masked, all the other characters masked as either comics or grotesques. The 'naturalistic' aspects to their roles are thus to some extent stylised – President or Schoolmaster – but become through that stylisation visual signs to match the clichés with which they express themselves. Valerio's expression is a mixture of the witty Touchstone and the sinister Jaques-like puppeteer, with slit eyes, a mop of dark black hair, and a huge, flat nose. Leonce, all in white with short black hair, is caught in a limbo world of figures dressed in black whose featureless faces are pointed solely by a few white lines or marks. The President suddenly becomes menacing in his sharply angled mask and pointed nose, and his white gloves lend a clinical nastiness to his manner. Valerio, in black, but with white stripes on his jacket to suggest an affinity with Leonce, perhaps, or a fool's motley, has bare feet, his one touch of humanity. He sits on an emblematic Chinese box, looking with closed eyes at the audience, against a neutral background without the least trace of naturalism. How powerful is this man? What does he know? The stylised wine bottle which he clutches to his chest seems to radiate a sinister power which none of the others can control.

King Peter himself has a tragic face, with huge, horse-like nostrils and the ruffs of a clown around his neck: but he has white gloves as well, which, with his hooded eye-lids, give him a predatory air. In the contradictions of the form he presents is the key to the contradictions of his mind and through the exploitation of such formal counterpoint the deep strength of the play is revealed. Mehring notes that the style he has adopted demands of the actor subordination of himself to his role, or mask. His voice and body thus become instruments of expression in the hands of the director in a manner similar, says Mehring, to stone and wood in the hands of a sculptor: and so the play is liberated from pedantic literalism.

Mehring's achievement was a production universally seen as definitive, showing how mime and more conventionally verbal theatre could combine as the best response to the two contradictory formal impulses, those of naturalism and the picaresque. If there is a disadvantage in his approach it is in making the work too existentialist, and not realist enough. As we see only one face, the contrast between the face and the mask becomes immensely powerful, and the demasking of the masked face a direct challenge to the face without mask, suggesting the face itself is a mask. But the danger is that the potentially limitless variation on face and mask takes the play off into a metaphysical speculation about appearance and reality rather than a statement about the brutal physicality of rags and hunger. Mehring has the peasants there, but as figures, rather than real people who by their appearance in an aristocratic 'masked ball' shatter the glittery illusions. The gain to compensate this loss of realism is that the class-centred diagnosis of social evil that Büchner offers is greatly reinforced by the fact that the aristocrats in their masks all seem to be limbs of the same shadowy body, covered from head to foot, inaccessible, untouchable. In this world Valerio's bare feet are a constant threat since they speak of 'nature' in a way that threatens to unmask 'art'.

The set of Jürgen Gosch's production in East Berlin is similar in some respects to Mehring's, a bleak, white room under white light, with a flight of steps at the front leading into the audience. Leonce is again all in white, and Valerio in black, though in sunglasses for a mask, which makes him

110

look more like a KGB hood than Touchstone. There is no luxury at all in this kingdom any more than in Paris: Rosetta is cut from the play and the production is designed solely to illustrate how unfit for high office is either Leonce or Valerio. Popo is no historical place, but East Berlin now, so that Leonce's weakness is a thinly veiled attack both on the Party, and on the East German intelligentsia's failure to constitute any effective opposition to the Party. The local press was naturally hostile, suspecting the production – but of course not the author! – of openly bourgeois and decadent tendencies, of a portrayal of Leonce and Lena as Vladimir and Estragon waiting in vain for the Socialist State. The public came in droves, which was probably another reason why the play was closed down well before the end of its run.

Gosch did not use 'epic' theatre techniques – placards, songs etc. – to make the immediacy of his production clear, but rather let Büchner's own portrayal of the failure of communication between rulers and ruled speak for itself, a point very sensitive in East Berlin, capital of perhaps the most repressive of all communist bloc regimes. This was brilliantly expressed in one addition to the 'props' list, though very much in harmony with them, the introduction of a plastic shopping net full of southern fruits as an emblem of all those sweet fruits of freedom forbidden to the audience. These fruits, in their bright colours, flashed tauntingly against a court where the king and counsellors, probably in conscious reference to Mehring's idea, are black and blind. They seem in fact like carrion crows waiting to pick the carcases of the dead, an image well understood by an audience familiar with official black suits and official black cars.

As well as touching a regime on the raw, this production surely pointed out how little a party man Büchner would

111

have been, however close his thinking was to that of the early communists, for his attack could work just as well in South Africa. It does however, underline the difficulty of getting the play's message across to those who have no direct experience of totalitarianism.

While in Paris and East Berlin *Leonce* self-evidently develops themes in *Danton,* in London it is seen simply as Büchner relaxing. Nick Hamm's production was hampered by a tiny stage and an equally tiny cast which meant most of the play's contrasts of size had to be sacrificed. The actors found particular difficulty having no 'through-line' of character to establish' and they had no external political situation to replace this. They tended therefore towards a more absurdist treatment of the play, which while very well acted, did not touch its political strength. This was not their fault: English actors are seldom trained in non-naturalistic acting methods and have little or no mime experience; and their audiences have a prevailing predilection for plot. What they did capture particularly well was the lyricism with which the play is in debate. But it is one of those anachronistic curiosities about Büchner in London that he can be praised by one critic for being like Beckett, while the true praise is the other way round.

6
Woyzeck

On 3 June 1821 the barber, wig-maker, sometime soldier and peasant farmer Johann Christian Woyzeck, then forty-one years old, murdered the forty-six-year-old widow of the surgeon Woost. He stabbed her seven times in the doorway of her house in the Sandgasse in Leipzig and she bled to death in a few minutes. Not long after the murder, Woyzeck was apprehended and confessed, and the case appeared closed. The immediate cause of the crime seemed to be jealousy: Woyzeck had had a relationship with the widow for some time, but he was far from the only man in her life. Though he knew this, on the day in question she had stood him up at short notice in favour of a soldier (she liked soldiers) and it was thought this had enraged him. But then it came out that he had bought the murder weapon, a broken sword blade, before the rendezvous was refused, and indeed had a handle fitted to it that afternoon. This changed the *crime passionel* theory into one of premeditated murder.

During questioning, it became evident that Woyzeck's

behaviour was not entirely 'normal' and Dr Clarus, medical adviser to the court, was asked to examine the prisoner with a view to a plea of diminished responsibility. Clarus presented his first report on 21 September 1821 in which he acknowledged Woyzeck's oddness but attributed it to the effects of 'strong liquors' and a 'lax life-style'. The execution was planned for November 1823 – the case took that long to go through – but was postponed after the court received another claim that Woyzeck was mentally disturbed. Clarus was asked to do his job again, a slightly strange decision, which he did, returning a second report on 28 February 1823 in which he confirmed his previous judgement.[1] On 27 August 1824, three years after the crime, Woyzeck was executed in front of a huge crowd in the main square at Leipzig, as a surviving print of the occasion shows.

If the slow process of judgement were not ample reason for doubting that justice had been done, the medical adviser to the Bamberg court, Dr Marc, raised medical doubts in his polemical pamphlet *Was the Murderer J. C. Woyzeck, executed on 27 August 1824 in Leipzig, responsible for his actions*? Clarus replied by publishing his two reports and the battle lines in what was to be a classic debate about criminal responsibility were drawn. Büchner's father had both documents in his own library and the case was certainly discussed in the family.

Perhaps even as early as 1835, though at the latest in the spring and summer of 1836 Büchner worked on this source material which he transformed into the *Woyzeck* scenes. Woost is made into the younger and more sensual Marie, though Marie also likes well-built soldiers; Woyzeck is changed from the disturbed but generally placid drunkard and misfit into a much more explosive, though not necessarily mad, barber and soldier; and their relationship is

114

made closer by the invention of their child, Büchner's single most important addition to the source. More significant than any such change is that for the first time in European theatre not the protagonist but the circumstances in which he lived, and ultimately society, are made the real causes of the crime committed. Woyzeck's tragic magnificence lies in his uncomprehending questioning of these causes, embodied for him in the persons of the Captain, the Doctor and the Drum-major who seduces Marie. '*Warum ist der Mensch?*', he asks, in his own version of Hamlet's 'What a piece of work is man?' Through such unanswered questions, Büchner indicts the historical Woyzeck's judges, indicts a society that could not understand, still less prevent, his predicament. But he does much more: the play's revolutionary scenic construction takes the experiments of the second and third acts of *Leonce* to their natural conclusion, to a work with almost no explicit logic, no classical *liaison des scènes,* only an inner, immanent dynamic that is ideally suited to the dislocated world it describes. This demands of the reader or audience an exceptional degree of willingness to participate actively in the process of dramatic reconstruction of Woyzeck's crime, and to see the scenes as evidence on which each spectator must make his own decision.

The Text

Few modern texts are more intrinsically problematic than *Woyzeck*. Until 1971 there was no authoritative interpretation of the handwritten manuscripts. The widely-read Oxford University Press translations, for example, are based on equally widely-read versions of the play by Fritz Bergemann, whom Lehmann, the 1971 editor, has shown to be inaccurate in any number of instances. A second problem is that the manuscripts, once correctly deciphered, leave no final scenic order so that the editor has, at least for the purposes of performance, to commit himself to decisions about the order of play. To illustrate the extent of the problem, I have summarised how the history of editing has produced radically different answers to this question, in comparing Lehmann's order with seven others, three of which are English translations.[2] The scenic strategy of *Woyzeck* is so anti-classical, based on a technique of nuance, balance and counterpoint, that there is no 'story-line' to which one can refer for help with the scenic arrangement.

There are two basic versions of the *Woyzeck* text, grouped under the headings of a 'provisional final draft', coded H4, and two groups of scenes belonging to the first draft, coded H1 and H2. A third group, coded H3, contains a variety of versions of scenes in the two main manuscript groups, but also has material not in either of them, including what Lehmann's edition makes the final scene, that between the fool, the child and Woyzeck.[3]

This textual complexity, and the hotly disputed scenic order make it unwise to attempt a plot summary. Since the play is short I hope I may be forgiven for not offering one.

The choice of scenic arrangement, and indeed the content of each scene is infinite in its possible permutation, placing a heavy responsibility on editor and director alike. I do not have the space to argue the case for Lehmann's edition in any great detail, but, as it is the one I find most satisfactory, I shall look at his choice of first and last scenes since the reasons for their selection explain by implication, the selection and order of the rest. What then is the first and last thing we should see?

The version of the play most regularly performed is based on Bergemann's edition and starts with Woyzeck

TABLE 6.1

	Lehmann (1971)/ Mackendrick (1979)	Franzos (1879)	Landau (1909)	Kupsch (1919)	Bergemann (1962)/ Price (1971)	Mueller (1963)
(1)	Open field: town in the distance. Woyzeck, Andres.	A room: Captain, Woyzeck. (5)	A room: Captain, Woyzeck. (5)	A room: Captain, Woyzeck. (5)	At the Captain's: Captain, Woyzeck. (5)	At the Captain's: Captain, Woyzeck. (5)
(2)	The town: Marie at window. Margreth, curfew march, Drum-Major, Woyzeck at window, the child.	Open square, Show booths (3a)	Open field: town in distance (1)	Doctor's Surgery. (8)	Open field: town in distance. (1)	Open country: town in distance. (1)
(3)	a) Show booths, lights, crowd. b) inside booth, Marie, Woyzeck, NCO, Drum-Major. (*Lehmann prints two scenes in all other editions as one*)	Inside booth. (3b)	The town. (2)	Open field: Town in distance. (1)	The town: Marie at window etc. (2)	The town: Marie at window. (2)
(4)	A room: Marie, Child, Woyzeck.	A room. (4)	Doctor's surgery (8)	The town (2)	Show booths, lights, crowd. (3a)	Entrance to fair. (3a)
(5)	At the Captain's: Woyzeck, Captain	The courtyard at the Doctor's (18)	Open square, booths. (3a)	Open square, booths. (3a)	Inside booth (3b)	Interior of booth. (3b)
(6)	Bedroom: Marie, Drum-major	Open field (1)	Inside booth (3b)	Inside booth (3b)	Marie's room (4)	Marie's room (4)

117

TABLE 6.1

	Lehmann (1971)/ Mackendrick (1979)	Franzos (1879)	Landau (1909)	Kupsch (1919)	Bergemann (1962)/ Price (1971)	Mueller (1963)
(7)	In the street: Marie, Woyzeck	The town (2)	The street (7)	The street (7)	At the doctor's (8)	At the doctor's (8)
(8)	At the doctor's: Doctor, Woyzeck.	Doctor's surgery (8)	Doctor's courtyard (18)	Doctor's courtyard (18)	Marie's bedroom (6)	Marie's bedroom (6)
(9)	Street: Captain, Doctor, Woyzeck.	Street (6)	A room (4)	Street (9)	Street (9)	Street (9)
(10)	Guardroom: Andres, Woyzeck.	Street (9)	Street (9)	A room (4)	Marie's room (7) (*Lehmann sets this scene in street*)	Marie's room (7)
(11)	An inn: Artisans, Woyzeck, Marie's dance. Drum major.	Marie's room (7)	Marie's room (7)	An inn (11)	Guardroom (10)	Guardhouse (10)
(12)	Open field: Woyzeck	Inn (11)	—	Marie's room (7)	Inn (11)	The inn (11)
(13)	Night: Andres, Woyzeck in same bed.	Guardhouse (10)	Guardhouse (10)	Guardhouse (10)	Open field (12)	Open field (12)
(14)	An inn: Drum Major, Woyzeck, crowd.	An inn (14)	An inn (14)	An inn (14)	A room in the barracks. (13)	A room in the barracks. (13)
(15)	Pawn shop: The Jew, Woyzeck.	Open field (12)	Open field (12)	Open field (12)	Doctor's courtyard (18)	Doctor's courtyard (18)
(16)	A room: Marie, Fool.	Barracks (13)	Barracks (13)	Barracks (13)	Barracks yard. (–) (*omitted by Lehmann*)	The inn: a scene with Woyzeck as Barber. *Only used by Mueller.*

(17)	Barracks: Andres, Woyzeck.	Barracks yard (–)	Barracks yard (–)	Barracks yard (–)	Barracks yard (–)	Barracks yard (–)	Inn (14)	Barracks yard (–)
(18)	Doctor's courtyard: Doctor, Students, Woyzeck.	Marie's room (16)	Marie's room (16)	Marie's room (16)	Barracks (17)	Pawn shop (15)	Pawn shop (15)	The inn (14)
(19)	Marie, Girls in front of her house, Grandmother	Pawn shop (15)	Pawn shop (15)	Pawn shop (15)	Marie's room (16)	Marie's room (16)	Marie's room (16)	Pawn shop (15)
(20)	Evening; Town in distance: Woyzeck, Marie.	Street (19) (grandmother)	Street (19) (grandmother)	Street (19) (grandmother)	Street (19) (grandmother)	Street (19) (grandmother)	Barracks (17)	Marie's room (16)
(21)	People come.	Barracks (17)	Barracks (17)	Barracks (17)	Pawn shop (15)	Barracks (17)	Street (19) (grandmother)	Open field (–) (*Mueller's edition only*)
(22)	The inn: Woyzeck, Käthe, Fool.	Woodland path by pond (20)	Woodland path by pond (20)	Woodland path by pond (20)	Woodland path by pond (20)	Woodland on the edge of a pond (20)	Woodland on the edge of a pond (20)	Barracks (17)
(23)	Evening; town in distance: Woyzeck	Inn (22)	Inn (22)	Inn (22)	Inn (22)	Inn (22)	Inn (22)	Street (19) (grandmother)
(24)	Woyzeck by a pond.	Woodland path by pond (23+24)	Woodland path by pond (23+24)	Woodland path by pond (23+24)	Woodland path by pond (23+24)	At the pond (23+24+21)	At the pond (23+24+21)	By pond (20+21)
(25)	Street: Children	Early morning, Marie's front door (*– this is not in Ms but a suggestion as to what Büchner might have done*) (27)	Early morning, Marie's front door (*– not in orig. Ms*) (27)	Early morning, Marie's front door (*– not in orig. Ms*) (27)	Early morning, Marie's front door (*– not in orig. Ms*) (27)	—	—	The inn (22)

TABLE 6.1

	Lehmann (1971)/ Mackendrick (1979)	Franzos (1879)	Landau (1909)	Kupsch (1919)	Bergemann (1962)/ Price (1971)	Mueller (1963)
(26)	Court official, Doctor, Judge.	Autopsy room (*– not in Ms but a suggestion based on*(26))	Autopsy room (*– not in Ms but a suggestion based on*(26))	Autopsy room (*– not in Ms but a suggestion based on*(26))	—	At the pond (23 + 24)
(27)	The fool, the child Woyzeck.	—	—	—	—	The street (25)
(28)	—	—	—	—	—	In front of Marie's house (27)
(29)	—	—	—	—	—	The morgue (*Here Mueller once again 'edits including Judge, Clerk, Policeman, Captain Doctor, Drum-major, Sergeant, Fool, Woyzeck, Marie's body.*)

Numbers thus (1) refer to the equivalent scene number in the Lehmann edition.

shaving the Captain, a scene in which Woyzeck himself plays only a secondary role: it ends with Woyzeck wading into the pond, following his knife deeper and deeper in towards death by drowning. This creates a quasi-naturalistic progression from Woyzeck the relatively normal, if subservient, army barber at the start, to Woyzeck the jealous murderer, to Woyzeck the remorseful suicide – a sort of lower-class *Othello*, which undoubtedly was one of the play's models. But the weaknesses of the arrangement are obvious: Büchner rejects at every opportunity tritely melodramatic and moral motives for the killing, so is this suicide legitimate either within the play or in the context of the beliefs we know Büchner to have held? Surely not. Likewise, there is plenty of evidence he was even thinking of taking the play as far as the trial, a further reason for rejecting the suicide. Lehmann, by contrast, starts with what is the first scene in the provisional final draft, in an open field where Woyzeck sees the bloody 'hedgehog'. Not only does this scene open the play in nature, as a firm counterpoint to the city world – that Sodom and Gomorrah – which brings Woyzeck down, but also makes the 'hedgehog-head' the first image that we encounter. From the start there is an image of severance, horror, blood and hallucination all of which fixes Woyzeck's emotional state before we see anything else. It acts, like the Weird Sisters in the first scene of *Macbeth*, as a point of reference for the rest of the work.

The Lehmann version closes with Woyzeck returning to the city, only to be spurned by the one person left with whom he has any relationship, his child. Far more disturbing than a suicide is this final gesture of alienation, making Woyzeck's life so empty that neither life nor death, still less justice or mercy, has any meaning for him. Remembering that Büchner invented the child, this would seem much more plausible an end, for it suspends both our judgement of his behaviour and indeed the end of the play, which is left hanging in an identical manner to the end of *Lenz*. Lehmann resists the trap of naturalism and of motives like jealousy and locates the play's movement within those natural forces of which Woyzeck's crime was a product.

When the shaving scene does come in Lehmann (scene 5) its resonances are much richer, and its ironies more accessible than at the beginning. If the Captain says 'Woyzeck, he has no morals' or 'you think too much' in the first scene we see, we have no way of assessing the status of his remarks, how truthful he is, what he means by 'morals' and thought. If, on the other hand, we have already seen a disturbed Woyzeck first on his own, and then with Marie, both remarks stand out as being the key issues of the play and the Captain by no means a figure whose judgement is to be trusted. For Büchner is asking us to consider what the implications are of such concepts as 'normal' behaviour, which in turn implies some norm of morality and logical thought: and he is not showing us a naturalistic, step-by-step alienation of a social misfit, but initiating us into what it feels like to be in alienating situations, the images and behaviour those situations induce. These situations are not, he is implying, a private vision of Woyzeck's but common to us all since they are a product of the society we have created and choose to live in. We need know little more about Woyzeck than that he sees bloody heads to grasp this point, but we must know it from the start.

A Structure of Oppositions

The tension between the field and the city, seen by Woyzeck burning in the distance, is central to Büchner's perception of both the physical and religious forces in the world. Nature, the field, simply is, with no moral or spiritual codes to assess its relative goodness. The city is man-made and stands not only for man's arrogant belief that he has overcome nature, but for all his absurd moral and spiritual card-houses which he builds to justify his arrogance. Around this structure of opposed energies, Büchner ranges a number of others which Lehmann's first scene illustrate. Andres sings the first of many folk-songs in the play, about two hares sitting and chewing the grass, which links the 'natural' poetry of the folk-song with the field and establishes a counterpoint between verse and prose and sung and spoken language. There is another opposition established when Woyzeck is suddenly afraid at Andres's silence, a fear which reminds us that drama is probably more about silence than sound.

The vision of the severed head, moving like a bloody hedgehog over the grass generates an opposition of a more metaphysical kind, between the real and the imagined and between the intellect and the heart from which it is severed. Woyzeck suspects the hands of the freemasons: the spectator may think of the severed heads of the guillotine or the Weird Sisters' apparition, each presaging bloody death.

From these initial oppositions Büchner builds an elaborate series of contrasts which is most readily visible in his choice of environments. As we saw in *Danton*, his interest was particularly in liminal scenes, those on the boundary of opposed states, and such are the scenes in *Woyzeck* in which the action progresses. The two basic physical states are the field with the town in the distance, and the enclosed space in the town – a bedroom, the guardroom, an inn, a fairground booth. These enclosed spaces are sub-divided, as in *Danton*, into the public and the private, and Woyzeck has difficulty expressing himself either verbally or physically in the public places.

There are several types of liminal scene: one such is set in the guardroom where Woyzeck shares a bed with Andres. Here a 'public' building is given a 'private' atmosphere by the bed, but contradictorily Woyzeck cannot communicate his fear to Andres, the one person who seems capable of understanding him. Another, the second scene of the play, is explicitly liminal: people are looking out of doors and windows at the passing curfew parade. From inside her window Marie sees the Drum-major for the first time, while Woyzeck, outside the window but not part of the parade, is in a doubly vulnerable state, belonging to neither world. In the following scene the threshold actually becomes the hinge of the action as the crowd is led from outside the show-booth to inside, rather as the audience in the theatre is 'led' into the action of the play. Much later on, the Grandmother tells her story in the doorway of a house.

Woyzeck's gradual alienation is mirrored in the way he is excluded from the private world of Marie's room and forced out into nature, caught for a while in the in-between state of the street and the guard-house. This sequence ends mid-way through the play in a very brief but crucial scene, set in a field:

> WOYZECK: Always at it! Always at it! Silence music! (*Presses himself against the earth.*) Hey! What! What did you say? Louder, louder – stab, stab the she-wolf dead? Stab the she-wolf dead? Shall I? Must I? Do I hear it there as well, is the wind saying it too? I hear it all the time, all the time, stab dead, dead.[4]

The positioning and purpose is similar to the central scene in *Danton* when Danton too lies on the ground, but here Büchner has added more explicit natural forces, the earth and the wind, as the 'motives' for the coming murder.

When Woyzeck does finally kill Marie it is, significantly at variance with the source, on the edge of a pond between the natural elements of water and wood, not in her doorway.

The effect on Woyzeck of this natural message is, as with Danton, a delirium and he wakes up Andres to ask for help. Andres tells him to drink gunpowder and brandy and go back to sleep. But Woyzeck is now under natural law and 'city' remedies are no use. To reinforce this, he starts to hear violins – in German drama a traditionally devilish sound – which reintroduces the register of music and reminds him of the seductive dance Marie performs for the Drum-major.

Music and dance are the two key forces in the environments of the inn and the fairground, though in both they have ambiguous meanings. Marie's dance is, much like Marion's speech on feeling, at the opposite end of the scale from Woyzeck's cramped gestures and sense of moral behaviour: it expresses her physicality and sexuality but equally her amorality since one purpose of the dance is to change partners. Yet at the same time, the dance in its naturalness suggests another type of natural energy, at odds with Woyzeck's, which is bound to come into conflict with his. On this perception rests the 'logic' of the play, as Anton Büchner noted in 1913: 'This destiny [Woyzeck's] passes on over us like a folk-song, not solely because of its many folk-song stanzas sprinkled into the text, but also because of the jerking, almost strophic technique of composition.'[5]

In the third scene of the play the important relationship between form and meaning as expressed through song and dance is made explicit when an old man turns a barrel organ while a young child dances, a motif which, curiously or not, ends Schubert's nearly contemporary song cycle *Die Winterreise*. The old man sings of death and Woyzeck comments: 'Poor man, old man! Poor child! Young child!

Sorrows and dancing!'[6] The song, and the scene, is breath-takingly simple and, like a folk-song, breathtakingly con-tradictory. Old men and children take places next to each other as naturally as death and dancing, so why, argues Büchner, cannot 'intellectual' and 'adult' concerns reflect this wisdom? Yet this is not a modish excitement at the creative genius of children and fools, but rather seeing in the pain and simplicity of the very young and very old and poor a natural, pragmatic understanding of life which they cannot express any other way than in simple songs. Marie, Andres, the young girls, Käthe, Woyzeck all sing songs, and the Grandmother tells a fairy tale. All of them tell the truth without pretention, because they tell it without being conscious of it. Their truths are not moral, or immoral, but simple natural facts on which lives are built. In one of the last letters Büchner wrote to Minna he asks her to learn more folk-songs, and one can see in *Woyzeck* how pro-foundly he understood the psychology of them. They both help create a context for the work in common experience and contrast obliquely with the world of human puppetry of the Captain and the Doctor. At the same time they under-line how indivisible drama and politics were for Büchner since the songs implicitly cry out for recognition of the common lot.

The fairground environment, framed as it is by death and dancing, introduces another of Büchner's favourite themes, that of the puppet, only this time the 'puppet' is a performing horse. Puppetry becomes an image of nature perverted by man:

SHOWMAN: Show your talent! Show off your animal powers of reason.[7]

At first, this horse has a Swiftian feel, a beast more reason-able than savage man. But then, as if Büchner were step-

ping back from the remark to a position of personal commentary, we are told 'the beast is unsullied nature, unidea-
lised nature. Learn from him! [. . .] That means: man be
natural. You are created of dust, sand and dirt. Do you
wish to be more than dust, sand and dirt?' The last question, so like Büchner's dying words, is a complex one. It
alludes to a passage in Lenz's play *The Soldiers* and it
directly echoes Büchner's letter from Strasbourg about the
Christmas fair, where the children long for the gaudy
mysteries of dust, sand and dirt – painted toys – which they
will never possess. Behind the allusions lies a philosophical
debate. Büchner is engaging intellectually with Christian
teaching, and annexing to his own beliefs certain Christian
propositions about human behaviour. He uses the showman to present an emblematic warning again the Vanity of
Human Wishes, one of the eighteenth-century Christian's
favourite themes. Yet, by giving the lines to the showman,
he also ironises their moral charge, not to ridicule but to
suggest a new, secular way of understanding what pride is.
Man is so proud of his reason he has now forgotten that he is
in essence animal.

The natural dignity of the animal suggests another line of
thought dear to Büchner – Rousseau's doctrine of the
'noble savage'. Both the animal and Woyzeck are on display: to earn money Woyzeck has contracted his body to
the Doctor and been required to live on a diet of peas. The
Doctor shows him off to his students much as the showman
displays the horse, implying as he does so that Woyzeck and
the horse were born, as the *Courier* says, on the fifth day to
serve the Doctor who was born on the sixth. So the display
of curious 'animals' becomes part of that same metaphor of
political exploitation which is set up in the *Courier* and the
whole play-within-a-play scene of the show-booth is suggestive of a satire on contemporary social relations.

Büchner is acutely conscious of the importance of such display and has the showman stress the point:

> *Die rapräsentation anfangen! Man mackt Anfang von Anfang. Es wird sogleich seyn das commencement von commencement.*

I have left the speech untranslated because of its blend of French and German and its dialect spellings, but it is clear that the showman's power, as the dramatist's, is both to 'represent' and to make 'beginnings', both of which qualities have political potential.

Creative power establishes a further level of debate with Christian thought. In the power of the dramatist to 'make' people is a contradiction of the claim that God made everything, or at least a further claim that each free individual is God to himself. The criminal injustice done to Woyzeck by society is the denial of that freedom because he is not of sufficient social standing to be allowed to exercise it. The only occasions when Woyzeck could be free were making love to Marie, surely an act of prayer for Woyzeck, and when he kills her, his one moment of self-realisation and free will. Büchner partially accepts Christian thought in his belief that to legislate for freedom and rights for such men as Woyzeck misses the real issue, which is that there is no substitute for love; but the love that Büchner advocates is not Christian but 'natural'.

This love is the one barrier between the intellectual and his becoming a 'puppeteer', an issue of Faustian proportions. Goethe's *Faust* was in fact one of the works Büchner studied most closely; for him its discussion of the power and limits of human knowledge, and the reaches of the human spirit defined the mental landscape of his whole generation. Faust the great thinker, with, significantly for Büchner, major scientific abilities, dissects the mind and sees into its recesses. In *Woyzeck*, Büchner is also anatomising a mind, and with it a world, observing its behaviour in a variety of situations, each scene describing one typical result. This smacks of the puppeteer, or of the Doctor's experiments, a charge which Büchner could only answer with love. As a dramatist he is confronted with the same feeling as Meister when reading Shakespeare, of opening a Pandora's box of strange and powerful emotions that can no longer be contained. He is in no sense guilty for having opened the box, and in any case natural human desire for knowledge – curiosity – explains, even justifies, his action. But he is also aware that he has powers which others do not, a realisation which in itself challenges at root the ideal of common good and common ownership. The only escape from this dilemma is in using one's talents for the common good, the practical application of natural love.

Woyzeck as parable?

There is no question Büchner wanted to teach with his last play, but what? *Woyzeck* is more skilful than *Danton* and its author consequently harder to find: the passage from the show scene which picks up the thoughts of one of his letters is in fact the work's only traceable allusion to his own nonfictional writing. This has meant critics have had a free hand in interpreting the play's purpose, and opinions are sharply divided. What critics tend to forget, however, is Büchner's own refusal of teleologies, of neat systems of interpretation: and when Büchner represents contradictory views in his plays it is often because he sensed them in himself. Taking into account the textual complexity, *Woyzeck* is about no more nor less than *Woyzeck*, an intrinsic part of which is contradiction. To support my view I shall examine three main readings of the play and indicate that it is their desire to make a complex work into a simple parable that invalidates them as they stand.

There are three distinct lines of thought, in many respects exclusive, which Kurt May in a much-reprinted article has summarised: the sociological and socio-historical; the tragedy of nihilism; and the theological (perhaps one should say 'anti-theological').[8] The first of these sees Woyzeck as the victim of an evil, exploitative society in which he is controlled by forces beyond his understanding, and for which he cannot be held responsible. Working from the premise that 'one is none' he is seen not as an individual but the member of an exploited class, an example of Marx's theory of the alienation of the working class. May claims that in this interpretation Woyzeck loses his central place in the tragedy, but this misses the point of the argument: Woyzeck is made to stand for the oppressed 95 per cent of the Hessian people quite deliberately. There is no reason why he cannot be both individual and representative at once: in the hands of a weak actor this will not work, but even the most rigidly applied rules of socialist theatre, in which the actor is required not to be but to observe his role, cannot prevent audiences developing affinities with the central consciousness of what they see. Just as a parable can support more than one kind of meaning, offering at least the literal and the spiritual alternatives to complement each other, so too can *Woyzeck*.

The second view, the tragedy of nihilism, sees *Woyzeck* as a study of a world in which there is no hope, an anticipation of the position Nietzsche explores in *The Birth of Tragedy*, that the best thing for a man is not to be born, and if born to die as soon as possible. Woyzeck matters as an individual only because the senselessness of his suffering illustrates the nihilistic case, and our sympathy for him is nipped in the bud by the awareness that it, too, is pointless. May again objects, arguing Büchner would not have written a play if he were a nihilist, since writing is optimistic by nature. He sees Woyzeck as rather purged, redeemed even, by suffering, a sort of Hessian Oedipus come to Colonus. But his argument is weak on two counts: he assumes, despite all Büchner's denials, that Büchner was morally inclined; and he advances the absurd proposition that one cannot write nihilistically. Nietzsche says that the only reason one does write is to resolve the problem of the pointlessness of life into the purpose of tragedy: and this is not an activity that springs from hope, but rather from necessity. In other words, *Woyzeck* warns us not to look for hope or meaning in life and that its only message is that it has none.

The third analysis is religious, developing the Oedipal analogy in the context of an unquestioning acceptance that Büchner's dying words are to be seen as a death-bed conversion which Woyzeck prefigures. May states: 'In Büchner's tragedy there is indeed a religious experience, but not that of a secret longing for Godhead, but rather that of a heavy pressure, an elementary fear, as in Woyzeck's premonition that God's will is indeed at work in the world.'[9] Little could be further from the truth than to see Woyzeck as intuiting the Hegelian World Spirit, though the wish to see God at work in Woyzeck's world is as understandable as the hope that *King Lear* ends with a turn for the better. The point of both works is that there is no such hope, no higher will or purpose: we have to find a way of coming to terms with what is simply nature. The necessary price we pay for being Gods of our own worlds is to face the realisation that any meaning we attribute to our lives is our own. Curt Sigmar Gutkind, after seeing Steinrück perform

Woyzeck in Frankfurt in 1919 approached the problem this way: 'And perhaps this work receives its supreme consecration when and because the individual reader or listener is forced, because the play is not fully rounded off, to add matter from his own soul's feelings and to mix with the blood of its imagination the colours of his own experience.'[10]

The Staging

Seeing *Woyzeck* on stage affirms Gutkind's view. Its remarkable 'myriad-mindedness' not only supports but demands a differentiated response from each individual spectator. Although 'parable' in the classical exegetic sense is not a suitable term to describe this special property of the work, if redefined against what we know of Büchner's beliefs it goes some way to expressing its capacity for supporting a range of complementary meanings. When interpreting a Bible story like the Good Samaritan, Christian commentators identify four levels of meaning in the text, the literal, the allegorical, the moral and the spiritual. *Woyzeck* may analogously be interpreted according to four levels of meaning, the literal, the metaphorical, the socio-political and the 'natural', where the 'natural' in Büchner's thought, as we have seen, occupies a place similar to the 'spiritual' in Christian teaching and with many similar properties. The crucial difference however, seen already in Büchner's disagreement with Weidig, is that while the Christian system takes the mind upwards towards God, Büchner's asks it to stay firmly in the here and now, something the physical actuality of theatre is particularly suited to exploring. I shall therefore consider how productions of the play may be located within the revised exegetic model I propose.

In a brief article written in 1947 Ingeborg Strudthoff, noting how after the end of the Second World War, *Woyzeck* was being performed again, describes three classic versions of the title role, starting from the thesis that 'in Büchner's works it is not people who act, but rather the work acts: it plays on the people like on so many instruments.'[11] The actors in question are Albert Steinrück, Eugen Klöpfer and Walter Franck, whose initial concepts of the role fit approximately the three theories that May examines.

The first, and perhaps greatest, of all Woyzecks was Albert Steinrück who first took the part under Eugen Kilian in Munich in 1913, a century after Büchner's birth. Anton Büchner, who saw Steinrück perform the same year in Berlin, this time at the *Lessingtheater* under Barnowsky, still remembers the vivid power of the performance; and, if contemporary reports may be believed, Steinrück was even more impressive the following year as he learned to master the demanding techniques of Bücherian acting. Steinrück had many great qualities: he was a large, powerful man, and in his strength, his head sunk taut over his shoulders as if poised for some great blow, he caught and suppressed Woyzeck into a trunk of coiled tension. His eyes by contrast were frightened, oppressed and in their maddened gaze were the Freemasons and the severed head. In the slight tilt of his head, his ears cocked, one heard as well the voices telling him to kill. His performance ranged itself therefore between the strength, energy, and even wit of his body and the hopeless vulnerability of the eyes, suggesting like Goethe's view of Hamlet, that Woyzeck was burdened with experiences beyond his mastering. When he bought the knife he was quite calm, bowing to an inevitable law, and when he said to Marie 'let's go. It's time' it was in a tone he might have used going shopping. Only after he has killed her does the coil inside him spring and with it comes all the revolt of his oppressed class. Strudthoff calls this version the 'socio-political' Büchner, and Woyzeck an embodiment of Büchner's own frustrated revolutionary energy; but I do not agree with her view that Woyzeck is here shown as intelligent as Büchner, nor does Anton Büchner who saw the performance. Rather there is a distinction which Steinrück exploits between his own consciousness of Woyzeck's position and Woyzeck's ignorance, the revolutionary message being the more powerful for Büchner's refusal to be explicit about it. Steinrück showed that the actor could maintain the two levels even within himself presenting a realist front with great stress on physicality to mask the political purpose.

Dictated by his much slighter build, Eugen Klöpfer's Woyzeck had less immediate physical presence and was more depressed, afraid of the world in which he lived and the large and splendid bodies of soldiers like the Drummajor. His performance drew as well on the effects on society of the Flanders war, investing Woyzeck with the insane energy of the shell-shocked mind. The director was again Barnowsky at the *Lessingtheater*, but the year 1920, the beginning of one of the greatest decades in German theatre. In 1921, Klöpfer directed himself in the role at the *Raimundtheater* in Vienna and then returned later in the same year to perform under Reinhardt in Berlin. Klöpfer's build made a naturalistic case-study of a mind under great stress possible in a way that Steinrück's did and his Woyzeck evolved into a companion piece to Lenz, portraying a man broken by circumstance. Yet, by a stroke of genius, Reinhardt was able to use this naturalism in a non-naturalistic way. For the first time he had *Woyzeck* performed on its own, a whole evening's entertainment, and between each scene he introduced long pauses. The resulting clash between naturalism in the acting and existentialism in the setting, between words and silence in equal balance, exposed more clearly the underlying nature-city opposition of the text. The binding element is the folk-song and accompanying music which suggest a structural principle derived from the narrative ballad. This *Woyzeck* Strudthoff terms 'poetic' and illustrates the second of May's categories, that of moral education: but by that token it challenges May's third, theological thesis, since this is not a world with a God, but one with men and what Woyzeck fears is other men.

The third Woyzeck, Walter Franck, grows out of Klöpfer's and presents precisely the nihilistic vision that May will not allow. In a production directed by Jürgen Fehling in Berlin in 1947, once again Woyzeck is charged with the energy of a war, though this time in a Berlin destroyed by Allied bombing and Russian artillery. The play describes loneliness, separation, severance from love and known values. Franck described his own performance as 'all sinew and no meat', but this implies that the spectator must flesh out the sinew in the same way demanded in Steinrück's interpretation. Woyzeck is largely passive, and not until the Drum-major throws a glass of beer in his face does he decide to act. By then the tension is too great to be controlled and he explodes in an ecstasy of creative destruction. A major difference in approach between Steinrück and Franck lay in their manner of delivery, Franck capturing the mood of laconic poetry that Steinrück suppressed, and allowing himself to be carried more by the text than Steinrück who stamped himself firmly on it. This more passive approach to Woyzeck leads naturally to Lehmann's version, allowing Woyzeck to drift hollowly after the murder, trying desperately still to communicate, and once again failing.

All three performances sustain my proposed four-fold

interpretation, though naturally with different emphases. The thrust of Steinrück's portrayal is to examine the tension between the natural level of meaning, which he represents in his body and the socio-political which one glimpses in his eyes, the literal being consciously suppressed and the metaphorical reserved for the one moment of the killing. Klöpfer's also uses the natural, but this time as a foil to the literal where simply in his size Woyzeck represents oppression. Because there is less tension between the literal and natural levels, the socio-political is suppressed into an aspect of the folk-song and the metaphoric located in the actual technique of staging with the long pauses between the scenes. Franck makes the natural and metaphorical levels coincide more closely through his particular emphasis on voice and his general consciousness of being an actor. He indicates that 'literal' meaning on the stage becomes *de facto* metaphoric and that it is the property of metaphor to have socio-political implications.

As is implicit in my choice of Woyzecks to describe the staging, the play depends essentially on how he is conceived: on that decision rest all the technical concerns. If one decides on naturalism, the play has a setting as constantly changing as *Danton* and the actor has the well-nigh impossible task of making a character out of a small number of lines. Irrespective of style *Woyzeck* has a large cast and potentially huge production costs, and tends to suffer from poor resources. Charles Marowitz, for example, directed it at London's Open Space in 1973 and his expanded text conflicted awkwardly with the confined stage-space. On the other hand, Tony Gash's decision at the Theatre Royal Studio, Norwich in March 1979 to conquer the cramped stage by including the auditorium in the action worked especially well for the fairground and the Doctor's waiting room, underlining the fact that the audience must make up its own mind about the Woyzeck case.

One reason why in English the work tends to become a sort of dramatised *Jude the Obscure* is the problem of translation. Woyzeck, as indeed most of the figures in the play, speaks dialect, the so-called *Hainer-deutsch* of the area around Darmstadt. While in Germany dialect does not necessarily carry a stigma, in England until recently it did and the result is a distinct poverty on stage in England of a dialect tradition that is not quaint. One obvious, but risky, solution would be to treat the play in the manner of Synge, in a specific Irish accent, or perhaps in Cornish, though here again industrial England has rather lost touch with an essentially rural mentality from which *Hainer-deutsch* comes. John Arden has often shown that dialect can work richly on the stage, so perhaps he could consider tackling *Woyzeck*.

7
A Man of Our Time

Büchner is an author whose works still feel unquestionably modern, but this very quality constitutes the biggest difficulty in describing his influence on other modern writers. In a gaffe, now famous in German theatre history, which illustrates this problem, a French critic of Jean Vilar's 1953 production of *Danton* criticises its author, evidently thinking the work to be brand new, for not taking account of the then most recent research into the French Revolution.[1]

The root of the problem lies in the fact that Büchner the writer of the 1830s created a series of figures who now, like Hamlet or Faustus, seem to represent modern types, or be modern myths. They face twentieth-century conflicts in what feel like twentieth-century ways: Danton, the successful revolutionary who suddenly asks himself, like Pasternak's Strelnikov, what he has achieved, and if indeed he, or rather natural forces, was the true agent; Leonce, the student prince, who, with more money and power than sense suddenly perceives the limits of his world without having the will or courage to change it; Lenz, the schizophrenic genius, who is driven out of the world by social pressures beyond his control; Woyzeck, the most arrestingly modern of all, who pictures man as an animal, living on or below the boundaries of human dignity, more through our fault than his. And then the women, deeply loving and yet passionately committed to their own emancipation, giving of themselves in ways a male-orientated world has still not learned to value.

Because Büchner's myths are very much ours, they grow in meaning because they grow with us. But for this reason it is hard to say whether later writers who describe similar types of experience do so under Büchner's influence or because they are sharing a common cultural awareness. Dietmar Goltschnigg has traced Büchnerian influences in nearly every major German writer since 1879.[2] I feel less convinced: Brecht for example refers to Büchner as one of the decisive influences on him, but this is hard to prove from the texts. Rather Büchner should be seen as a writer whose influence is so extensive because he embodies two qualities modern authors aspire to emulate: he wrote works that have the power of self-renewal and he wrote in an immediately recognisable style.

Phases of Stage History and Literary Reception

The literary reception of Büchner's work began a generation before the theatrical, largely for financial reasons. *Danton,* for example, costs far too much to risk on stage without first having the guarantee of a solid base of interest from a potential audience. Once this interest had been established, however, both the literary and the theatrical reception proceeded at great pace and in the ten years from 1911, when the stage renaissance started, to 1921, Büchner went from a minor unknown to a classic of the German theatre. Now it is no surprise to find *Woyzeck* starting the 1980 Hamburg season, *Danton* being a major première in the 1980 Munich summer and Berg's opera *Wozzeck* a major attraction at the 1980 Edinburgh festival.

The phases in Büchner's rise may be defined as from his death till 1879; from 1879 to 1945, breaking at 1933; and from 1945 to the present. The first of these is in a sense paradoxical in that nothing happened in it, but the reasons for his neglect are in part the reasons for his rediscovery. The second phase has many sub-divisions, the most important of which was the obvious effect Hitler's rise had on German theatre. And the third phase may well turn out to be misleading since research into his work is now so intense that any hope of maintaining familiarity with all of it has long gone.

(i) *1837–1879*

In his exhaustive history of the Mannheim National Theatre from 1779–1929, Ernst Leopold Stahl analyses the most popular playwrights at that theatre in a number of statistical tables, which, as Mannheim was one of the most important and best attended houses in Germany in the whole period, may be taken as reasonably typical of tastes.[3] In the fifty years 1839–1889, which very nearly corresponds to the first phase of Büchner reception, Schiller, after the ubiquitous Kotzebue, is by far the most performed playwright, followed at a distance by Goethe, Shakespeare and Lessing. Such was Schiller's dominance over the whole period of Stahl's history that the three single most popular works were *Wilhelm Tell, Kabale und Liebe*, and *Die Räuber*, which I referred to earlier.

The crucial importance of Büchner's relationship with Schiller entered a new phase with Büchner's death. Ingeborg Strudthoff summarised the problem as follows:

'The resistance to Büchner could be called Schiller. Since the development of the classical theatre in Weimar, Schiller's views on tragedy, as found expressed in the practice of his works, and thereby the shadow of Kant were dominant on the stage.'[4] What Schiller and Kant stood for were moral codes and imperatives of the sort Büchner rejected outright. The failure of Büchner's works to establish themselves in the nineteenth century must be seen as a direct result of his refusal of such codes. For where Schiller, under Kant's influence, preached the triumph of freedom over necessity, Büchner argues the reverse; and although there are grounds for seeing their positions as complementary not exclusive, it was always Schiller who took the honours in the theatrical lists.

But Schiller and all he stood for were not the only hurdles in the way of Büchner's work. His plays set directors and technicians acute problems of construction and coordination. *Danton* has a huge cast to drill and no less than 32, often complex, scene changes for the technical staff to accomplish. It was, significantly, only after the introduction into the theatre of such technical innovations as the electrically powered revolving stage, the treadmill and electric lighting during the 1880s and 1890s that such tasks became feasible at the sort of speed the action demanded. Even then, it took some twenty years for directors to learn how to rethink their production strategies to include technology, the first major figure to do so being Max Reinhardt who revolutionised German staging technique in the years following his appointment to the *Deutsches Theater* in Berlin in 1905. It was Reinhardt who really established Büchner's reputation with the broad theatre-going public.

(ii) *1879–1945*
The moral and technical barriers which Büchner faced were

compounded by the lack of a readily available edition of all his work until 1879. When this deficiency was rectified its effect on those who read his plays, like Gerhard Hauptmann, was electrifying. So began the twenty-year process in which the leading practitioners of German-language theatre were educated in Büchnerian technique. Both they and their audiences had to be lured away from grandiose diets of Wagner and a notion that the theatre was a place of celebration of Germanic mythic strength – in either case, no easy matter. Theatres ultimately depend on their audiences and to understand the size of the task facing Büchner's work one must also understand the nature of the audience he had to convince.

Typical to this day of the financing of German theatre is a huge, politically sensitive subsidy and a so-called *Abonnement* ticket system where seats for a whole season are sold in advance. In Mannheim, for example, this system had an enduring tradition. All the major local families bought their regular block of tickets but also had the same seats handed down over generations as part of the family inheritance. The social structure of the city could be read from the seat arrangement, the higher up the theatre, the lower one's status. The inevitable result was that the court, and the well-to-do families in the Grand Tier had a major say in who had what post and what plays were shown.[5]

All this changed in the social upheavals before and during the First World War during which Büchner sprang into prominence. Suddenly German society was facing problems it had suppressed for a century: when seen from the perspective of the Flanders mud the world was senseless, savage and hideously indifferent to the individual. Young, shattered people saw in Büchner's plays experiences which they knew at first hand, the pain, the turbulence and the ultimate resignation. This turbulence, and later this resignation also characterised German political life after the war, from the heady days of the attempted communist coup in Bavaria in 1919 to the dole queues and inflation of the 1920's which brought Hitler to power. Just how greatly this benefited an understanding of Büchner's work is illustrated by the fact that from 1909–1920 no less than five complete and fourteen individual editions of his work were published, with *Danton* (seven editions) leading the field by a wide margin.

This especial interest in *Danton* points to the dominance of the 'political' Büchner at least until 1933. *Woyzeck* and *Leonce and Lena* were played a good deal – often together – but it was the supposed political message of *Danton* about which argument was most fierce. Then after 1933, at first of necessity but then more by choice, the 'poetic' Büchner, which the perceptive director Eugen Kilian had noticed as early as 1911, asserted itself more. On this rising tide *Woyzeck* has come, rightly, to be seen as the richer play. What was clearly established however, by 1945, was that both 'political' and 'poetic' approaches to Büchner could work on stage and that actors, given time, could master the necessary techniques without having to 'rewrite' the original for performance.

(iii) *1945–1980*

Since 1945 the case for Büchner does not have to be made as such, but outside Germany it is still hard to find authentic texts in performance. It will take time especially for all the new information about *Woyzeck* to seep through onto the stages of the world.[6] Just as the experiences of 1914–18 enabled audiences to grasp the significance of *Danton* so the memories of Auschwitz and Hiroshima make it easier for us to understand the full extent of the alienation and disorientation of *Woyzeck*. My hope is that we shall come back to Franzos's view, expressed as early as 1867, that what makes Büchner so fascinating is that he is both 'political' and 'poetic' at once and that *Leonce and Lena* may be the beneficiary of that further shift in perception.

Works Inspired by Büchner

The adventurous and brief life that Büchner led has been the subject of a number of writings about him, grouped around the flight from Darmstadt and the death. Goltschnigg has traced seven poems, eleven stories, three novels and four plays in German alone, though the great majority are of little intrinsic merit. But in such examples as Georg Herwegh's poem, two lines of which are on Büchner's memorial stone in Zürich, and Kasimir Edschmid's fine novel about both Weidig and Büchner – *A German Revolution* – there is evidence that Büchner can inspire work of a high quality. In some ways it is surprising that such an exciting story as the *Courier* affair has not been turned into a cloak and dagger film.

Richer than most of the works about Büchner's life have been those that turn his material into another medium. The outstanding example is Alban Berg's opera *Wozzeck* which had its première at the *Berliner Staatsoper* on 14 December 1925 under Erich Kleiber. So successful has this work been that internationally it is probably better known than the play on which it is based: and it has also been a contributing factor in establishing the play's reputation world-wide. Seldom have words and music corresponded so well without such a radical alteration to the source as, say, those of Boito for Verdi's Shakespeare operas. Hans Mayer who was at the première recounts: 'Much about the deepest individuality of this poetry and its poet appeared once more in a new form and another language [. . .] Nowhere is Büchner's relationship with the common people better

understood than here [. . .] The music succeeds in bringing
final clarity to the last of the mysteries [. . .]'[7] Nor was
Berg's the only opera of the time based on *Woyzeck:* a
second was written in 1926 by Manfred Gurlitt, of which the
libretto is most interesting. (I have not seen the score.)
Striking about Berg's choice of *Woyzeck* is also its affinity
with his opera *Lulu*, based on Frank Wedekind's play of the
same name. Wedekind admits that it was Büchner's work
that first sparked him to write and Berg's selection further
underlines the affinity between these two great playwrights.

Film and television have been less successful than opera
in touching Büchner. Certainly the editing table makes it
easy to conquer the problems of elaborate set changes, but
film, for all its ability to take the audience close up to the
performers lacks the concentration on the physical
presence of the actor which Büchner's work demands. The
most recent attempt at a film, Werner Herzog's *Woyzeck*,
with Klaus Kinsky as Woyzeck and Eva Matthes as Marie,
would also suggest it is not just a question of film technique.
As an actor, Kinsky brings to his role something of a
mixture between Walter Franck and Eugen Klöpfer: but
his portrayal comes across as altogether too intelligent and
articulate, a sort of Dorian Gray after seeing his own picture rather than a Hessian peasant. His performance is
further defused, or perhaps diffused, by too much emphasis
on the beauties of the Hessian landscape which has about it
the naturalism of a travel film. Marie was physically convincing but her preference of a rather weak Drum-major
over a highly intense and attractive Woyzeck seemed
implausible, notably in the crucial dancing scene. Perhaps
the answer to the problem of filming Büchner is that his
work, to steal Marshall McLuhan's terms, is 'hot' only on
stage and 'cool' on film.

Büchner's German Influence

After 1879 it is hard to find a major literary figure in the German speaking world who does not claim to be in Büchner's debt, and in the mid 1920s for example, Büchner had become so dominant that young writers began to protest that his reputation was stifling theirs. Even today a young German playwright will tend to measure himself, at least as a young man, against Büchner's achievement. Frank Wedekind, Gerhart Hauptmann, Bertolt Brecht, Ernst Toller, Hugo von Hofmannsthal, Ödön von Horvath, Max Frisch, Friedrich Dürenmatt, Peter Weiss, Carl Zuckmayer and Thomas Bernhard have all been through the Büchner 'school' and the range of their work is a sign of how widely Büchner's influence has spread in both 'political' and 'poetic' theatre.

Successful though his theatre is in stimulating political debate, his plays fit awkwardly into the frame defined by Brecht and Walter Benjamin as 'epic' theatre and even more awkwardly into the monolithic class-based structure of literature towards which many recent Eastern European critics of high party standing have tried to lead him. (One of the few works to be published by the Russian revolutionary presses in the abortive attempt of 1905 was Büchner's *Danton*.) Büchner the hater of totalitarian systems would surely have been purged by Stalin and would find himself today on the side of the non-Christian dissident. His work does however, share with 'epic' theatre one essential characteristic, the use of the *gestus*.[8] This most elusive of modern theatrical terms has at its heart the notion that theatre should not falsify history in its presentation of past events by rewriting it to fit some artistic ideal of plot. From this it is argued that a *gestus* should be the representation of an historical action or idea as truthfully as possible and as ideas, or at least words, are easier to pervert and distort than actions, that the emphasis of the theatrical presentation should be on action. The length of a *gestus* may be a brief theatrical moment, or a whole play. *Woyzeck* as a whole may be seen as a *gestus,* while the use of the guillotine or Marion's speech are more specialised examples from *Danton.* The test of the *gestus* should be its immediate and unmistakeable truth according to the lights of common experience. Instead of seeing Büchner's works as embodiments of modern myths one could argue that they are classic *gestus.* Büchner is probably more successful an exponent of this technique than those whom we now regard as its discoverers. Büchner's historical accuracy in *Danton* exposes the glaring falsifications of much socialist theatre (remember East German official displeasure at the very accurate production of *Leonce and Lena*) and is not guilty of the charge that Theodor Adorno levels at Brecht's *Arturo Ui* and *Mother Courage* that they both belittle and falsify the historical issues with which they deal. This truthfulness will continue to make Büchner controversial and unpopular in totalitarian and repressive societies.

While the 'epic' writers tend to draw on Büchner's political strategies, his structural innovations and his documentary style, the expressionists like Edschmid appeal more to the intensity and sympathy of his creative method. This stems foremost from *Lenz* but clearly is evident in Woyzeck and Danton as characters. Frank Csokor's *In Memoriam Georg Büchner* talks personally to Büchner about the intensity of the feeling he had for his subjects and asks him if he wrote in his own blood; and other poets, like Siegfried von Vegesack, have seen in this self-sacrificing a type of Orphic blood-letting which through the death of its author brings the life of the created work. In prose perhaps the best example of successful interaction between an author and Büchner is Robert Walser's story *Büchner's Flight*:

Black, great, wildly strewn clouds often covered the moon, as if they wanted to lock him up, or wanted to throttle him, but every time he stepped out of the darkness again, like a beautiful child with enquiring eyes, towards the peaks and freedom, casting rays of light about him on the silent world.

The equation of Büchner with the moon, with its suggestion of both serenity and yet vulnerability reflects a depth of understanding with its subject comparable to Büchner's own with Lenz.

The most problematic area of Büchner's influence is his language, to which all writers who praise him refer with awe. In its terse and explosive energy, its naturalness and its metaphoric richness it has no equal in the German theatre. There are passages of similar strength in Goethe and Brecht, but no writer can sustain such intensity for so long. Büchner's language is also politically potent, full of manifesto-like statements of the kind one finds in Marx and Engel's *Communist Manifesto*. Long before the Dadaists claimed 'art is a weapon' Büchner had realised this aim in his art and made it a weapon for social change. To this end he also drew on documentary sources, using as much as possible from authentic material to underline the historical truth of what he was describing. This pointed the way for Piscator and Brecht in their development of 'epic' theatre and stimulated Reinhardt to one of his finest productions – *Danton*. Underlying the linguistic energy and innovation is another Büchnerian strength, the ability to generate a language that is specific to each new text. For this reason his style is both suggestive and hard to emulate, for it demands not imitation or allusion, but rather analogy. Each writer must do his subject the justice of creating for it its own specific language.

In summary: many writers refer with gratitude to Büchner, but his gift to them is more as muse than model. This is not to underestimate the linguistic and stylistic influence Büchner has had but to warn that there are few if any 'Büchnerians'. The inspiration he drew from Büchner is what Wedekind meant when he said to Wilhelm Herzog: 'without *Woyzeck* . . . his first drama *Spring Awakening* would not have come to being.' For this same quality Brecht placed Büchner in a direct line that led from Shakespeare through Lessing to his own time.

Influences Outside Germany

On stage Büchner has been performed regularly in the West since the 1920s, especially so after 1945 when he represented a type of German literature that did not smack of the Thousand Year Reich. But his work has been victim both of well-meaning attempts to rewrite it and of the fact that Fritz Bergemann's inaccurate texts have been the basis of most translations and performance copies. The result can be that when accurate translation is offered it is thought to be the opposite by those whose knowledge of the original is either limited or non-existent.

Where Büchner was caught in Schiller's shadow inside Germany, outside it has been Brecht's to put him in the shade, since by an irony of history the master came more slowly to the public attention than the pupil. While Brecht, for questionable reasons, has become almost revered in the public mind, even jostling with Shakespeare for first place in the school play stakes (though for the one good reason that he is easier to translate and there are excellent texts available) Büchner is still greeted with quizzical glances and requests for more information. Yet the climate is changing.

One British author, perhaps the best of our living playwrights, comes particularly to mind as in a Büchnerian tradition, not least because he has faced the same difficulties with the theatre establishment as Büchner, John Arden. In works like *Live Like Pigs, Sergeant Musgrave's Dance, The Workhouse Donkey* and most recently the *Non-Stop Connolly Show* Arden confronts the same sort of socio-political problems as Büchner with a similar blend of documentary and metaphor, of high and folk style. His structural technique – more conscious perhaps than Büchner's – has a shared interest in profoundly anarchic modes of expression as the only way to shake audiences free from their preconceptions about the role and subject matter of theatre. This is nowhere better expressed than in the Song of the Workhouse Donkey:

> O what a shock, I nearly died,
> I saw my ears as small as these,
> Two feet, two hands, a pair of knees,
> My eyeballs jumped from side to side,
> I jumped right round, I bawled out loud,
> You lousy liars, I've found you out!
> I know now why you're fleeing . . .
> I am no donkey never was,
> I'm a naked human being.

The cry is one that echoes throughout the *Hessian Peasant Courier* and the song is one that *Woyzeck* is always on the edge of singing: indeed, Butterthwaite who sings it has much in common with both Danton and Woyzeck.

Though not with Arden's genius, David Storey's work tends more towards the expressionist interest in Büchner as a writer who sacrifices himself to make art, and who sees the creative process as one of deconstructing and reconstructing the self. Storey is also, like Büchner, both play-wright and novelist and very much concerned with the special properties of genre and levels of discourse. His central characters all undergo experiences similar to those in *Lenz* and Allott, the art teacher in *Life-Class*, may stand for them all:

> Violation they tell me, is a prerequisite of art . . . disruption of prevailing values . . . reintegration in another form entirely.

This could well be a comment on Büchner's art.

The English-speaking theatre scene now appears to be more open to intellectual and political theatre than at any time since the Elizabethan and Jacobean stage and this must bode well for Büchner: it is only to be hoped that actors, directors, readers and spectators will face the challenge set them by Büchner's original conceptions.

References

1. A Brief Life

1. I have used throughout the text edited by Werner R. Lehmann, the *Hamburger Ausgabe*, 4 vols (1967–), hereafter referred to as Lehmann.

2. See, for example, Jochen Golz, 'Die Naturphilo-sophischen Anschauungen Georg Büchners', in *Zeitschrift der Friedrich Schiller Universität* Jena 13 (1/1964), pp. 65–72.

3. A photographic reproduction of this warrant is available in Ernst Johann, *Georg Büchner*, p. 151.

4. The argument is in Thomas Mayer's introduction to *Text und Kritik: Georg Büchner* (1979). The portrait is reproduced on the front cover of the book.

5. For the history of Darmstadt to the present see Eckhart G. Franz, *Darmstadts Geschichte* (Darmstadt, 1980), which includes a chapter on Büchner and the Vormärz.

6. For the achievements of all Büchner's brothers and sisters see Anton Büchner, *Die Familie Büchner* (1963).

7. Luise Büchner, *Ein Dichter*, ed. Anton Büchner (1964), pp. 23–4.

8. Ibid, pp. 40–1.

9. For an excellent review of political life in Strasbourg see Hans Mayer, *Georg Büchner und seine Zeit* (1946) pp. 232–40.

10. Lehmann II, p. 416.

References

11. An excellent survey of the history of the period is Jacques Droz, *Europe between Revolutions 1815–1848*, (1967).

12. Lehmann II, pp. 425–6.

13. Ibid, p. 427.

14. For a comprehensive study of this relationship see Thomas Mayer's study in *Text und Kritik*.

15. For a brilliant reconstruction of the mind of this man see Kasimir Edschmid's novel, *Georg Büchner: Eine Deutsche Revolution*.

16. Lehmann II, pp. 434–5.

17. Ibid, pp. 435–6.

18. Ibid, pp.490–1.

19. A useful anthology of 'Young German' writing is *Das Junge Deutschland*, ed. Jost Hermand (Stuttgart, 1972) (Reclam UB 8703–07).

20. Lehmann II, p. 462.

21. Ibid, p. 463.

22. Caroline Schulz's *Diary* is only available so far in Fritz Bergemann's edition of Büchner's work. These words were apparently spoken on 16 February.

2. A man out of his time

1. The power and influence Hegel exerted can hardly be over emphasised. See especially *Philosophie der Geschichte* in the edition of F. Brunsträd (Stuttgart, 1961, Reclam UB 4887–85), p. 595. All quotations from this edition.

2. *Philosophie der Geschichte*, 'Introduction', p. 50.

3. This is a brief summary of many ideas in the 'Introduction', but see p. 128.

4. *Philosophie der Geschichte*, p. 61.

5. F. König, *Georg Büchner's Danton*, p. 77 argues this case well.

6. *Philosophie der Geschichte*, pp. 78–9.

7. For the discussion of the 'Welthistorisches Individuum' see Ibid, pp. 74ff.

8. Ibid, p. 605. This is the concluding sentence of the whole work.

9. Lehmann II, pp. 34ff.

10. See Karl-Georg Faber 'Die Südlichen Rheinlande', *Rheinische Geschichte* (1979), vol. III, p. 388. The report also stresses the huge number of petty thefts of food.

11. Hegel refers to this document in *Philosophie der Geschichte*, in the context of a full discussion of the Revolution.

12. Lehmann II, p. 59.

13. Ibid, p. 43.

14. Lehmann I, p. 79.

15. Ibid, pp. 79–80.

16. Ibid, p. 82.

17. Ibid, p. 85.

18. Ibid, p. 86–7.

19. Ibid, p. 86.

20. Ibid, pp. 436ff.

21. Lehmann II, p. 153.

22. Lehmann I, p. 48 (3, 1).

23. Ibid, p. 49 (3, 1).

3. A tradition of dissent

1. A useful introduction to Lessing is by Wolfgang Drews, *Lessing* (1962).

2. *Briefe die neuste Literatur betreffend*, VII, den 16 Februar 1759. 'Siebzehnter Brief' printed in *Gotthold Ephraim Lessings Sämtliche Schriften* (23 vols), 2nd ed., ed. Franz Muncker (Stuttgart, 1886) vol. VIII, p. 42.

3. Ibid.

4. *Hamburgische Dramaturgie*, 'Vierzehntes Stück', den 16 Junius 1767 Muncker, vol. IX, p. 239.

5. J. W. Goethe, *Dichtung und Wahrheit*, VII Buch, in *Goethes Werke* (Hamburger Ausgabe) 14 vols, vol. IX, pp. 279–281.

6. J. M. Lenz, *Anmerkungen übers Theater* (1774); (Stuttgart, 1979), p. 9 (Reclam UB 9815). Hereafter referred to as *Anmerkungen*.

7. A useful introduction to Schiller's life and works is by Friedrich Burschell, *Schiller* (1958). See also Thomas Carlyle's *Life of Schiller*, 2nd edn (1845).

8. Quoted Burschell, *Schiller*, p. 31.

9. Friedrich Schiller, *Werke* (Hanser Ausgabe) 3 vols (München, 1966), I, p. 65. Just this question is picked up by Hegel in *Philosophie der Geschichte* in reference to Schiller. See esp. 'Introduction', p. 70.

10. J. M. R. Lenz, 'Über die Veränderung des Theaters im Shakespear' in *Anmerkungen*, p. 108.

11. C. D. Grabbe, *Napoleon oder die Hundert Tage* (Stuttgart, 1977), (Reclam UB 258), pp. 72–3. Hereafter referred to as *Napoleon*.

12. Lehmann II, p. 413.

13. *Napoleon*, p. 91.

14. Ibid, p. 91.

15. C. D. Grabbe, *Scherz, Satire, Ironie und tiefere Bedeutung* (Stuttgart 1974, Reclam UB 397), p. 4.

16. Ibid, p. 65.

17. Ibid, p. 18.

18. Ibid, p. 31.

19. Ibid, p. 32.

20. Ibid, p. 54.

21. I am indebted to Gerhard Fricke and Volker Klotz, *Geschichte der deutschen Literatur* (15th edn) (Hamburg, 1971), p. 144.

22. See the essay on 'Shakespeare' in *Von Deutscher Art und Kunst* (1773).

23. The most rewarding English version of *Meister* is by Thomas Carlyle.

24. Goethe, *Wilhelm Meister: Die Lehrjahre*, Book IV, ch. xiii, *Werke*, VII, p. 246.

25. *Lehrjahre*, Book V, ch. vii. Ibid, p. 307.

26. I am indebted here to Norbert Oellers, 'Geschichte der Literatur in den Rheinlanden seit 1815', in *Rheinische Geschichte* (1979), vol. II, pp. 582ff.

27. For statistical information on this subject see Eda Sagarra, *Tradition and Revolution: German Literature and Society 1830–90*, p. 96, and the tables at the end of Ernst Leopold Stahl, *Das Mannheimer National Theater* (Mannheim, 1929) pp. 383–423.

28. Franz Grillparzer, *Diaries 1839–40*, printed in *Sämtliche Werke* (Darmstadt, 1964) vol. III, p. 860.

4. Danton's Death

1. There is a useful summary of material on Danton relevant to the play in *Georg Büchner Dantons Tod: Erläuterungen und Dokumente*, ed. Josef Jansen (Reclam UB 8104) (Stuttgart 1969).

2. Goethe, *Campagne in Frankreich* (1822) *Werke*, X, p. 235.

3.   The translation is from the Everyman edition (1963) p. 21.
4.   Quoted in Hans-Martin Sass, *Feuerbach* (1978) p. 39.
5.   Sass, *Feuerbach*, p. 62.
6.   'Thought is in its original form merely a dialogue between me and another. Question and answer are the first factors of thought.' Quoted Sass, *Feuerbach*, p. 66.
7.   Lehmann II, p 443.
8.   In Hessian dialect Büchner's name would have been pronounced like Georges in French.
9.   Lehmann II, p. 292.
10.   Hans Mayer, *Georg Büchner und Seine Zeit*, pp. 182ff.
11.   Printed in the *Allgemeine Zeitung*, 5 Sept. 1957.
12.   Printed in the *Darmstadter Echo* of that date.
13.   Karl-Heinz Bohrer wrote an excellent, though highly critical review of this production on 25 April 1978 in the *Frankfurter Allgemeine Zeitung*.
14.   Lehmann II, pp. 425–6. This use of 'must' is also a conscious echo of Hegel in *Philosophie der Geschichte* and the theory of a 'necessary' progress to world history.

5. Leonce and Lena

1.   Hans Mayer, *Büchner*, p. 310.
2.   Here I disagree with Mayer.
3.   This is according to Thomas Mayer's dating in *Text und Kritik*, p. 411.
4.   Lehmann I, p. 116.
5.   Quoted in Armin Renker, *Georg Büchner und das Lustpiel der Romantik* (1924), p. 59.
6.   Lehmann I, p. 107.
7.   Ibid, p. 108.
8.   Ibid, p. 110.
9.   Ibid, p. 110.
10.   Ibid, p. 111.
11.   Ibid, p. 112.
12.   Stage direction, ibid, p. 114.
13.   Ibid, p. 118.
14.   Ibid, p. 119.
15.   Ibid, p. 119.
16.   Ibid, p. 120.
17.   Ibid, pp. 124–5.

18. Compare with Lessing's statement above, ch. 3 p. 38.
19. Lehmann I, p. 134.
20. Ibid, p. 133.

6. Woyzeck

1. The two reports, in reverse order, were published in Henke's *Zeitschrift für die Staatsarzneikunde*, a periodical to which Büchner's father subscribed. The texts are reprinted by Lehmann I, pp. 485–549.

2. In recent years sorting out the order of the *Woyzeck* scenes has become almost as much a critical and scholarly issue as Linear B. For further suggestions see Walter Hinderer's excellent *Büchner Kommentar*, pp. 182–3. Most important here is the fact that Lehmann (1968) agrees with Meinerts (1963) and Müller-Seidel (1964) that the work begins in the field.

3. Here I use Lehmann's coding: there are others.

4. Lehmann I, p. 422.

5. I am much indebted to Anton Büchner for providing me with a copy of this lecture which, I regret, was not published despite playing a significant part in the play's success in both Darmstadt and Heidelberg at that time.

6. Lehmann I, p. 411.

7. Ibid, p. 412.

8. Kurt May, 'Woyzeck', in *Das Deutsche Drama: Vom Realismus bis zur Gegenwart*, ed. Benno von Wiese (1975).

9. May, 'Woyzeck', p. 95.

10. Printed in *Rheinische Thalia*, Wochenschrift des Mannheimer Nationaltheaters, vol. III, no. 3, September 1922.

11. Ingeborg Strudthoff, *Berliner Hefte*, 5, 1947, p. 371.

7. A man of our time

1. See Paul Ellmar, 'Büchner schlägt Rekorde: Dantons Tod zum ersten mal in Paris', *Die Zeit*, Thursday 28 May 1953.

2. Dietmar Goltschnigg, *Rezeptions- und Wirkungsgeschichte Georg Büchners* (1975). My disagreement with Goltschnigg should not belittle my considerable debt to his work.

3. Particularly valuable are the statistical tables. See Stahl, *Das Mannheimer National Theater*, pp. 383–423.

4. Ingeborg Strudthoff, *Die Rezeption Georg Büchners durch das Deutsche Theater* (1957), p. 8.

5. See Stahl, *Die Geschichte . . .*, p. 15.

6. Even the 1972 translations by Michael Hamburger, while mentioning Lehmann's suggested scenic order, do not follow it on the thinnest of pretexts that the play is thus left hanging, which is surely what was closer to Büchner's understanding of Woyzeck than as remorseful suicide. The only English version which does follow Lehmann is John Mackendrick's (1979).

7. Mayer, *Georg Büchner und seine Zeit*, pp. 395–6.

8. See Walter Benjamin's discussion of this in *Versuche über Brecht*.

Select Bibliography

A Büchner
(i) Texts: German

Sämtliche Werke und handschriftlicher Nachlaß, edited and introduced by Karl Emil Franzos (Frankfurt/Main: J. D. Sauerländer, 1879).

Sämtliche Werke und Briefe, ed. Fritz Bergemann (Leipzig: Insel Verlag, 1922).

Gesammelte Werke, ed. and introduced by Kasimir Edschmid (München, 1948).

Sämtliche Werke und Briefe (Hamburger Ausgabe), ed. with critical commentary by Werner R. Lehmann (4 vols) (Christian Wegner Verlag Hamburg 1967–   ) (incomplete as yet). The standard edition.

(ii) Translations and English language editions

Dantons Tod and Woyzeck, ed. with notes by Margaret Jacobs (Manchester University Press, 1954).

Danton's Death, trans. John Holmstrom in *Modern Theatre,* vol. 5, ed. Eric Bentley (New York, 1957).

Complete Plays and Prose, trans. Carl Richard Mueller (Mermaid, New York, 1963).

Georg Büchner

Danton's Death, An English version by James Maxwell (Methuen, 1968) (a totally unreliable text).
The Plays, trans. Victor Price (Oxford University Press, 1971).
Leonce and Lena, Lenz, Woyzeck, trans. Michael Hamburger (Chicago University Press, 1972).
Woyzeck, trans. John Mackendrick (using the Lehmann text for the first time) (Methuen, London, 1979).
'*Leonce und Lena' and Lenz*, ed. M. B. Benn (Harrap, 1963).

(iii) Bibliographies

W. Schlick, *Büchner Bibliographie bis 1965* (Georg Olms, Hildesheim, 1968).
Gerhard P. Knapp 'Kommentierte Bibliographie zu Georg Büchner' in *Text und Kritik Georg Büchner*, I/II (München, 1979).

(iv) Reference and Criticism

Heinz Ludwig Arnold (ed.) and Thomas Michael Mayer *Text und Kritik Georg Büchner* I/II (München, 1979) (This contains vast amounts of new material).★
Maurice Benn, *The Drama of Revolt A Critical Study of Georg Büchner* (Cambridge University Press, London, 1976).
Lothar Bornscheuer, *Georg Büchner Woyzeck. Erläuterungen und Dokumente* (Reclam UB 8117, Stuttgart, 1972).
Anton Büchner, *Die Familie Georg Büchners* (Edward Roetner Verlag (Darmstadt, 1963) (Hessische Beiträge zur deutschen Literatur) .
Luise Büchner, *Ein Dichter*, ed. Anton Büchner (Darmstädter Schriften 17, Darmstadt, 1964).
Dietmar Goltschnigg, *Rezeptions- und Wirkungsgeschichte Georg Büchners* (Scriptor Verlag, Kronberg/Ts 1975). (Monographien Literaturwissenschaft 22).
Walter Hinderer, *Büchner: Kommentar zum dichterischen Werk* (Winkler, München, 1977).★
Josef Jansen, *Georg Büchner Dantons Tod. Erläuterungen und Dokumente*(Reclam UB 6060, Stuttgart, 1969).
Ernst Johann, *Büchner* (Rororo, Hamburg 1958).★
Arthur H. J. Knight, *Georg Büchner* (Oxford, 1951).

160

Select Bibliography

Hans Mayer, *Georg Büchner und seine Zeit* (Limes, Weisbaden, 1946).

David G. Richards, *Georg Büchner and the Birth of the Modern Drama* (Albany, 1977).

Ingeborg Strudthoff, *Die Rezeption Georg Büchners durch das Deutsche Theater* (Theater and Drama 19, Berlin, 1957).

(Works marked ★ contain useful bibliographies)

B GENERAL: Works of a background and introductory nature

Friedrich Burschell, *Friedrich Schiller* (Rororo, Hamburg, 1958).

Wolfgang Drews, *Lessing* (Rororo, Hamburg, 1962).

Jacques Droz, *Europe Between Revolutions 1815–48* (Fontana, London, 1967).

Norman Hampson, *The First European Revolution* (Thames & Hudson, London, 1969).

Eda Sagarra, *Tradition and Revolution: German Literature and Society 1830–90* (Weidenfeld, London, 1971).

Hans Martin Sass, *Ludwig Feuerbach* (Rororo, Hamburg, 1978).

David Thomson, *Europe Since Napoleon* (Pelican, 1966).

Benno von Wiese (ed.), *Das Deutsche Drama vom Realismus bis zur Gegenwart* (Düsseldorf, 1975).

– *Die Deutsche Tragödie*, Von Lessing bis Hebbel (8th ed.) (Hamburg, 1973).

Brief Chronology

1813 Born 17 October in Goddelau, a village near Darmstadt.

1816 Family moves to Darmstadt: father becomes doctor at the court of Grand Duke Ludwig I.

1822 Starts private school.

1825 Begins at Gymnasium (High School).

1830 *Cato* speech (defence of suicide) as end-of-year dissertation.

1831 Summer: leaves school.

9 November: matriculates at University of Strasbourg as medical student.

4 December: Polish nationalist General, Ramorino, visits Strasbourg – the subject of Büchner's first extant letter home.

1832 Gives talk to student club Eugenia on political conditions in Germany.

1833 2 April: attempted putsch in Frankfurt. Fiery letter to his parents on violence.

Secret engagement to Minna, daughter of Pastor Jaeglé in whose house he has been studying in Strasbourg.

31 October: matriculates at Hessian university of Giessen, but falls ill and returns home.

1834 January: returns to Giessen, meets Weidig and joins the pastor's radical circle.

March: founds the Giessen branch of the Society of the Rights of Man.

End March: finishes the draft of the *Hessian Peasant Courier* (*Der Hessische Landbote*) with statistical information provided by Weidig.

End April: forms Darmstadt branch of Society for Rights of Man.

July: Courier in print and circulated. Conspiratorial meeting at Badenburg.

August: Minnigerode arrested in possession of *Courier*. Büchner travels to Offenbach to warn others. His rooms searched in Giessen by Georgi, first meeting with Georgi.

End August: returns home to virtual house arrest.

1835 Police informer Konrad Kuhl begins to feed police information about Büchner's role in the *Courier*.

Jan-Feb: five weeks of work on *Danton*. Sends MS to 'Young German' Karl Gutzkow, who recommends it to Sauerländer.

9 March: leaves for Strasbourg, without passport. Exile begins.

Summer: translates Victor Hugo's *Lucretia Borgia* and *Maria Tudor* into German.

Starts work on *Lenz* and on scientific doctorate on the *Nervous System of the Barbel*

1836 Spring: gives three highly regarded lectures on his fish research.

Summer: writes *Leonce and Lena* and works on philosophy – especially on Descartes, Spinoza and the Greeks. Concerned about space and matter, and freedom, suicide and atheism.

September: given his doctorate by University of Zürich.

18 October: moves to Zürich.

November: trial lecture on the *Nerves of the Skull*, then appointed Reader in Comparative Anatomy. First drafts of *Woyzeck*.

1837 Further work on *Woyzeck*.

2 February: Start of illness.

19 February: Dies of typhus.

21 February: Buried.

Index

Index

Index

Index